Praise for
EVERYTHING IS NEGOTIABLE

"I didn't just read this book, I clung to it. Every page, every word. Anyone searching for encouragement and light will find it in this book."

—Jennifer Roup, @Thats_What_She_Read

"[Morgan] shows us how to get out of our own way and negotiate what we need to succeed in the moment and over time….when you expand your view of what is negotiable you create choices for yourself in the world. This book will help you do so."

—Deborah M. Kolb, PhD., author of *Negotiating at Work* and *The Shadow Negotiation*

"Put equal parts Nora Ephron and Dale Carnegie in a blender. Hit frappe. Enjoy the results. The name of this creation is *Everything Is Negotiable*. Consume immediately."

—Jeff Martin, Founder of Magic City Books, author of *My Dog Ate My Nobel Prize,* and editor of *The Customer is Always Wrong: The Retail Chronicles*

"Dr. Morgan's mix of personal experience from her life and experience as a professor and mentor are insightful, thought providing and often hilarious. I find myself going back to the 'Five Tactics to Negotiate for Your Life' again and again."

—Kathy Taylor, former Tulsa Mayor

Everything Is Negotiable

Everything Is Negotiable

The **5** Tactics to Get What You Want in Life, Love & Work

by Meg Myers Morgan, PhD

SEAL PRESS

Seal Press
Hachette Book Group
1290 Avenue of the Americas, New York, NY 10104
www.sealpress.com
@sealpress

Printed in the United States of America

First Edition

Published by Seal Press, an imprint of Perseus Books, LLC, a subsidiary of Hachette Book Group, Inc. The Seal Press name and logo is a trademark of the Hachette Book Group.

The publisher is not responsible for websites (or their content) that are not owned by the publisher.

Print book interior design by Six Red Marbles Inc.

Certain names have been changed and some individuals are composites.

Library of Congress Cataloging-in-Publication Data

Names: Morgan, Meg Myers, author.
Title: Everything is negotiable: the 5 tactics to get what you want in life, love, and work / by Meg Myers Morgan, PhD.
Description: Berkeley : Seal Press, [2018] | Includes bibliographical references.
Identifiers: LCCN 2018013052 (print) | LCCN 2018027864 (ebook) |
    ISBN 9781580057905 (e-book) | ISBN 9781580057899 (pbk.)
Subjects: LCSH: Negotiation. | Psychology, Applied. | Self-realization.
Classification: LCC BF637.N4 (ebook) | LCC BF637.N4 M67 2018 (print) |
    DDC 158/.5—dc23
LC record available at https://lccn.loc.gov/2018013052

ISBNs: 978-1-58005-789-9 (paperback), 978-1-58005-790-5 (e-book)

LSC-C

10 9 8 7 6 5 4 3 2 1

To the students, with gratitude.
Especially Cassandra Rigsby.

"Everything is negotiable. Whether or not the negotiation is easy is another thing."

—CARRIE FISHER

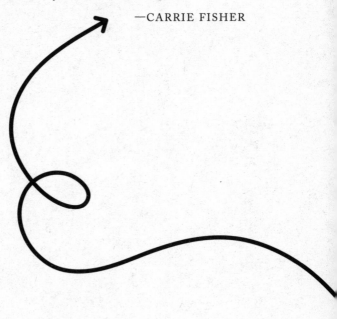

CONTENTS

Contents

Contents

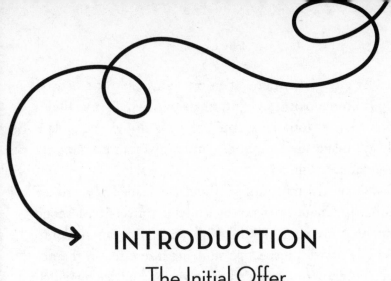

INTRODUCTION
The Initial Offer

My older daughter, Lowery, is six years old. When you meet her, you might be fooled by her white tendrils and angelic smile, but that girl is a shrewd negotiator, and I've learned a lot watching her craft. When she was younger, one of her many tactics was to convince my husband and me to let her reserve something for later if we wouldn't let her have it in the moment. She'd ask for a cookie. The answer was usually no. She'd nod respectfully, but then ask for the same thing in a different way: Could she put a cookie on the table? When we inquired why she wanted to do this, she explained that perhaps later, maybe after dinner, it would be okay for her to have a cookie, and if it was, the cookie would be ready for her. This tactic was (and still is) surprisingly effective.

At any given moment in our house, our kitchen table is littered with toys and treats over which my child is in current negotiations. And yet, by bedtime, the table is always magically cleared of clutter. She's an example for women everywhere.

As an assistant professor and the leader of a professional graduate program at a major university, I spend much of my time talking with and coaching students. Whether with prospective students interested in the degree program or current students seeking advice on which courses to take next semester, almost every talk turns into a deeper conversation about where their lives are headed. For years I have listened to people talk through their goals in life. Graduate school is often the compounding aspect of a student's life. They have a home life, sometimes filled with a spouse and children, and they have a professional life, often one of great responsibility. Adding school on top of all that tends to make anxieties, concerns, and dreams bubble to the surface. I just happen to be there when they do. These are often vulnerable concepts to acknowledge and verbalize, and I work hard to listen and advise well. This, by the way, is the greatest part of my job. I'm always catching people in the middle of a journey (or contemplating a journey) to better themselves. Students, after all, are just people trying to curate a good life for themselves, and their struggles and experiences are a microcosm for what a lot of ambitious people—students or not—struggle with.

Of the many students I've advised over the years, my female students tend to visit my office most often. I once thought this was because women tend to seek out other women for advice. But the longer I've had the role, the more I've come to realize that women tend to analyze their opportunities and assess their own value differently than men. That is to say, in broad generalities, women are *negotiating* more.

I don't mean to imply men don't struggle, compromise, or negotiate. They do. But I find male students don't *negotiate with themselves* in the way my female students do. Sure, much of this is societal conditioning and exposure to a generation of Adam Sandler movies. But men and women think about themselves, their lives, and achieving their goals in vastly different ways. This thought disparity often arises when I meet individually with people who are considering the graduate program I administer. In an average week, I talk with at least three people who have expressed interest in the program. Men tend to get straight to the point: They want this degree, they have confirmed with their peers it is a good idea, and they have a plan for what they will do with the degree when they graduate. Very rarely do men ask me about balancing the demands of graduate school with their professional and personal lives. Few, if any, ask about the rigor of the program or what the current student population is like, and never has a male prospective student said he was thinking of having kids, which might make going back to school complicated. In fact, their questions are almost always confined to the technical aspects of the program, beyond the decision—cost, schedule, and timeline.

Women, on the other hand, typically begin our meetings by enumerating all the reasons taking on a graduate program at this time probably won't work—they want kids soon; they are busy at their jobs; they need to devote time to friends and loved ones. Though they are often more excited by the prospect of graduate school than are their male counterparts, they are also more convinced there are too many obstacles in their way—obstacles that, I often uncover, are mostly self-imposed. And very rarely are the obstacles keeping them from achieving their dreams.

These general differences between men and women are, well, just that, but I continually notice this pattern emerge after countless meetings with prospective students and years of mentoring current students. As a result, I find myself constantly listening to the thoughts of women. My female students have trusted me with their concerns, not just over course schedules and class assignments, but over marriage, motherhood, educational and professional goals, and the battles they fight with their own sense of self-worth. I've heard nearly everything imaginable in my office, from "I'm pregnant!" and "I got a job offer!" to "I think I want to leave my husband" and, harrowingly, "I'm suicidal."

You see, the women I mentor are in the middle of a negotiation. I don't mean a salary negotiation—though we do a lot of preparation for that, too. I mean they are in the middle of a *life* negotiation, negotiating for the lives they want. Often, these women are negotiating with themselves, and somehow they are losing. I feel equipped to help my students negotiate because, well, I gave birth to the expert. As I said, my daughter is a shrewd negotiator, and she's taught me some powerful strategies that I pass on to my female students as they negotiate for the lives they want.

Given my experience with listening to women and coaching them to negotiate better with themselves, I was offered the chance to give a TEDx Talk for the university where I work. The university's TEDx team wanted me to shed some light on the struggles my students—particularly my female students—face. In that talk I outlined three tactics for negotiating for the life you want.

In this book, I expand and expound on those ideas. I outline five negotiating tactics I've learned from my strong-willed daughter that might help you negotiate for your life. I'm not specifically talking about negotiating for a promotion or a better price on a new house (though do try both of those!). Instead, I'm urging you, when you start to take some of your own wants and dreams off the table, to change the terms. I'm suggesting that when you start to undervalue your worth, up your own ante. If you are not wholly satisfied with the offer—the one that either you have been given or have given yourself—counter back. To successfully negotiate anything, however, you must first understand how much is up for negotiation. When my sister bought her first house, she demanded that the patio furniture be included in the sale. Having never bought a house myself, I was surprised by her stipulation because I didn't realize what all *could* be negotiated. But that's what you must realize when you look at each aspect of your life—from your career, to your relationships, to the way you feel about yourself: Everything is negotiable. Even the patio furniture.

If you can get clear in your mind what it is you want and believe it is yours to get, you will be successful. My daughter's understanding that everything is up for negotiation is why she's nearly always successful at getting what she wants. And you can get everything you want, too. To help you do that, I've outlined five tactics to clarify your wants, tame your fears, overcome your own hang-ups, and successfully walk away with the life and career you want, having outmaneuvered your wiliest opponent: yourself.

Five Tactics to Negotiate for Your Life

1. Don't Confuse Your Wants

You aren't going to achieve what you want in life if you aren't certain what it is you want. Most people get wrapped up in the wants of others, in competing with others, and in comparing themselves to others, and they lose sight of what they want. When it comes to life goals, don't be confused by others about what you want. Unless it's a haircut. It's hard not to want the haircuts of others.

2. Choose All That Apply

You've probably been told you have to make choices. You do, of course. But you've probably also been told that making choices means eliminating other great options. This makes no

---

sense, of course, because the more choices you make in life, the more choices you are presented. Ever made the choice to order a coffee at Starbucks? Then you get the concept.

3. Own the Terms

Ever have a date order your meal for you? Even if he or she orders what you wanted, you still feel weird, right? Well, we give over our narrative to more than just weird dates; we give it over in life—to our kids, our parents, our friends, our spouses. We let other people set our terms, often in small ways we don't even notice. You not only have to set your own terms, you must constantly communicate those terms. And you'll have the chicken, thank you very much.

4. Never Give Your All

I'll never understand where the concept "give it your all" came from. I'm guessing from a nurse in the delivery room. But by and large, very rarely do you need to give anything your all. See, buying into the idea that you must give anything and everything your *all* is what is holding you back from taking on new challenges. Who wants to start a new career path or go back to college when they are in the middle of streaming *House of Cards*? But if you know you don't have to give any of those your all, then all of it is possible.

5. Get Out of Your Way

More than anyone else, any schedule, any demand, and any obstacle, *we* are in our own way. Most of the time, we are in our heads thinking thoughts and dreaming up issues that will never come to be. And even if they do, there is no reward for having predicted the bad stuff, and no surefire way to ensure the good stuff. When it comes to getting what you want out of life, you'll find the biggest thing standing in your way is *you*. So step aside.

WANTING

TACTIC ONE

Don't Confuse Your Wants

I was cautioned that when my second daughter, London, was born, my older daughter would become jealous. Lowery would suddenly have to compete for resources that had always been solely hers. Everything I read, and every seasoned mother, warned me about how competitive siblings can be, especially two little girls. After London's birth, I braced myself for sibling rivalry and female competition.

Don't let my Instagram account—brimming with syrupy pictures of sisterly love—fool you. There certainly were (and still are) times my two daughters competed for my attention. But over time, I began to see they weren't really competitors. Lowery couldn't have cared less about this little red dinosaur we have until she saw London

3

wanting to play with it. Then Lowery would immediately engage in a cutthroat battle over something she had not cared about five minutes earlier. She wasn't competing for it, but she seemed to think she should.

One day I saw Lowery reconcile this as she watched her baby sister play with the red dinosaur. She looked around the playroom and realized all the other toys were up for grabs—toys that actually interested her. From that point forward—as best a young kid can—she stopped confusing her wants with her sister's.

Women are expected to compete with one another. Darwin figured this out way back when while sitting idly by and watching female chimps claw at each other over that one male monkey throwing his feces. Or something like that. And since then there has been an entire field of study devoted to understanding the territorial competition among females. Social researchers T. J. Wade and S. McCrea conducted a study in 1999 trying to gauge the response women might have when looking at attractive women. Female participants looked at pictures of other women who varied in physical attributes, like breast and waist size. They concluded that women exhibited a physiological response, as if threatened, when looking at pictures of perceived attractiveness. Their responses were based on looks alone. It's not like they had the IQ scores or cooking samples from the women in the pictures. After all, the most attractive female gets the best mate (although sitcoms in the 1990s and early 2000s—such as *Married with Children*, *King of Queens*, and *According to Jim*—seem to say otherwise). Anyway, this competition is so engrained in women—and primarily based on physical traits—that we are essentially trained to size one another up instantly as competitors.

But over the years of mentoring women and watching my two daughters get along better than anticipated, I've come to realize we women aren't in competition with one another. A competition implies we are vying for the same goal, *mutually* and *equally* engaged in a struggle for the exact same thing.

I know a lot of women. I'm friends with women. I teach women. I'm raising two little women. I see women walking around. And I've never once seen two women trying to do the *exact* same thing. Not once. All of my female students are roughly the same age and are pursuing the same specific degree, yet they do not have the same personal goals or career aspirations. No two women are ever trying to achieve the exact same thing. I mean, rarely are there even two women running for president in the same election year. And even then, it's never on the same side. So if we aren't competing, what are we doing?

We are *comparing*. And that's a much more dangerous thing because comparison sets arbitrary metrics for our life and often creates random deadlines for when life experiences should happen. Comparisons trick you into confusing your wants with someone else's.

A few semesters ago, I had a student in my office who had just started the program, and she told me, in no uncertain terms, that she needed to complete graduate school as quickly as possible. When I asked why she wanted to speed the process up, she explained that she had to graduate quickly so that she could have kids by the time she's thirty. Now, I didn't have her full medical chart in front of me, so I couldn't speak to the possible reasons for her timeline. But, in retrospect, I would guess she was looking around at her friends and placing an arbitrary deadline on her life. In other words, she was confusing her wants with someone else's.

When I first became a mother, I was suddenly—overwhelmingly—out of my element. My parenting in that first year was based almost exclusively on what I saw other mothers doing. One mom made persuasive claims about the importance, benefits, and *sheer joy* of making her own organic baby food. My interpretation of that at the time was that if I wanted my child to have a shot at Harvard, I'd need a hand mixer.

So that first year—despite my being a full-time doctoral student and an adjunct professor—you could find me at home for hours on end, (ignoring my child) in the kitchen, elbow deep in farmer's market squash—sautéing it, pureeing it, blending it, pouring it, and serving it up to my six-month-old, who would immediately spit it out in disgust. But I repeated that process over and over because *this* was important.

Then one day I was in the grocery store, and I don't know if I just don't ever look around, but can you imagine what I saw? Jars and jars and jars of organic baby food. Aisles of this stuff. I picked up a jar and studied the baby on the label, a very happy, well-adjusted look-ing, Harvard-bound baby. And I thought, *Wait, what am I doing?* What I was doing was spending an inordinate amount of time on something that was never a priority for me. I had looked around at another mother and immediately become entrenched in something I had never cared about before. There is not a distant version of myself that couldn't wait to blend avocado and rhubarb in a BPA-free container. I don't even like to cook.

But I was comparing myself to these other mothers, and it set me up for failure because I didn't have the same goals as these women. Not in parenting, and not in life. But that feeling, that knee-jerk reaction of panic and pressure—I have to *do* more, *be* more—crops up in other aspects of my life, not just parenting. I feel it in my professional life, especially as a female in academia.

When I first took a faculty position at a major university, I was incredibly intimidated. I was new and young (and female!), and I had no idea what was going to constitute success in the job. So I looked to those around me: professors who were decades into their careers, with publications and awards that took up pages and pages of their CVs. For nearly a year I stressed about living up to their standards, completely ignoring that I had been hired to save and grow a dwindling graduate program—no one else around me was there to do that. All of us at the university had completely different goals, not just in our job descriptions, but in our own professional ambitions.

When I started to have some success with that specific program, something I didn't expect happened: I became a threat to those who threatened me. It wasn't too long into my time at the university that I began to hear some grumbling about the attention my program was getting, or—maybe more accurately—the attention *I* was getting. During the first few years, I felt like I was running to catch up to all the academic giants around me—to even be considered a peer—only to turn around one day and see those giants wanting a little of what I had earned.

The turning point came when I recognized that I didn't want the career of a peer I admired just because she had great credentials. I wanted a career that I had built and that made sense for my personal and professional goals. But it is hard not to look at other scholars or mothers and *not* feel intimidated or immediately compare myself. So I must constantly keep in mind what my plans are for my career and for my life. I can't get bogged down in comparison because I'll confuse my wants with someone else's.

So how do we keep from confusing our wants? After all, sometimes we want something because we actually *want* it. And though our wants may be governed by various things like our peers, society, and *Gossip Girl* reruns, there are a few checkpoints to keep in mind when you are trying to figure out your wants.

YOUR WANTS ARE ALL YOURS

Competition among women is the nastiest stereotype of all. Gendered conditioning to see one another as the enemy is a big barrier we all face. My mother once told me, "Women don't dress for men; they dress for other women." I laughed because I was, like, seven, and I wasn't quite ready to absorb such wisdom. But I learned soon enough. When I was in junior high, I arrived at school one morning in my favorite outfit, a seersucker plaid jumper (I was hella cool). When I walked up to a large group of students standing outside the classroom, a girl named Alicia turned around, looked me over, and loudly said for all to hear, "Meg, you've already worn that this week." Now, evolution would point to the fact that as a junior higher, Alicia was set up to see my twelve-year-old bod cloaked in breathable plaid as a threat to her ability to attract a mate. At the time it was a tall, swarthy boy named Mark. Six months later we had all moved on to a short, blond, athletic kid named Wes.

But for the rest of junior high, I was overly stressed about how often I should wear an outfit. Was twice a month too much? I didn't have that many clothes. I fretted about this to varying degrees all the way up until I got married, and then I came to realize that men—particularly the man I married—were not that invested in what I wore. One evening, I was putting on makeup in our bedroom while my husband was struggling with his tie. We were preparing for a nice dinner out. A few minutes later I joined him downstairs. "Oh," he said. "You changed. I really liked the dress you had on earlier." I looked at him, befuddled, and said, "That was my bathrobe." Throughout my entire life, I was conditioned to believe women were competing with one another's physical attractiveness for a mate. But then, my actual mate didn't even seem to notice my outfit. What the hell?

So we spend our time thinking we are in competition with women. And, although we aren't really in competition, here's the trouble with thinking we are. In 2016, a couple of economics professors at the University of Amsterdam conducted a study looking at what happens to women who compete in the Math Olympics. They drew two interesting conclusions from studying the women as they competed: 1) Women are less likely to keep competing if they aren't getting positive feedback; and 2) They are more likely to stop competing after a setback. Yikes. This means that unless women are both being praised *and* winning, they are more likely to give up in the competition.

That's problematic for a couple of reasons. First, this study implies—perhaps rightly so—that women need positive reinforcement. I know that if my children don't "ooh" and "ahh" over a meal I cook, there's a stronger likelihood I might never feed them again. But the second concern is that women are giving up when they face setbacks like a loss. Yet, as I said before, women aren't competing in life. So you can't technically lose! Now, if you perceive you are competing, at some point you're probably going to perceive yourself as the loser. And then what? You. Will. Give. Up.

Studies like this might help explain why women don't go as far as men in fields such as academia or corporate leadership. And we bring that weird competition into other parts of our lives, too—like parenting, or skin care. And when we feel we are not measuring up, we back down. This is some bullshit. We are not competing! Wear your plaid jumpers!

It's been a long time since junior high, and I've made plenty of interesting fashion choices along the way. I've also had an abundance of female friendships that remind me we are not in competition. I find the women around me in my professional life to be incredibly supportive and encouraging. But I'm still susceptible to steering into the stereotype. Allow me to elaborate:

• • •

I first met Melissa at the open house for the preschool our children attended. At the time, the director of the school hosted a dinner for incoming parents to ease them through the tumultuous transition from maternity leave to full-time childcare. The event was arranged so parents could drop off their infants in one of the classrooms where three teachers eagerly awaited and then shuffle into the dining hall to meet other shell-shocked and sleep-deprived new parents.

Melissa and her husband showed up a little late. She had her newborn son, Jack, pressed tightly to her chest. All the other parents—especially me—were ecstatic at the thought of free childcare for an hour, and we had happily dropped our babies and run. But not Melissa. She had her son in her arms, looking lovingly down at him as he blinked up at her.

At the time, our babies were mere weeks old. I was in the darkest period of postpartum depression, having long given up the ability to nurse, and I was still struggling mightily to bond with my child. Watching Melissa effortlessly cuddle and nurse her baby—the only mother in the packed room to reject the available childcare—I decided definitively that I hated her.

I tried to avoid her after that night. When I saw her in the halls during morning drop-off, I cringed. She would so carefully and lovingly place her precious son in the teacher's arms, hand over a bucket of breast milk, and float effortlessly out of the room accompanied by blue-birds and field mice.

I would awkwardly hand over my child, leave her portions of formula, and slink out of the room, wondering whether I should have held my kid longer or brought a warmer blanket. Six years and two children later, mothering is now natural, fun, and fulfilling. But in the beginning, every aspect of it felt monumental, and I struggled to adapt. Especially the part in which I fully realized the depth of female competition.

Yes, I had my fair share of this in junior high. But being a woman never registered as anything other than the annual pap smear and picking a brand of tampons. When I became a mother, however, my eyes were opened to the two greatest downfalls of our sex: intra-gender competition, and salads as a meal.

Oddly, these two aren't unrelated.

In fact, most women suffer from both syndromes in a chicken-or-the-egg fashion. Although I assume competition came first because I think it is somehow hardwired into women. Eating rabbit food is a learned behavior.

Our perceived competition with one another is something society has thrust upon us (exhibit A: any cover of any fashion mag; exhibit B: all other aspects of life). We've been conditioned to believe there is an ideal image of us—how we look, live, mother, and marry. If we are presented the ideal image and we see another woman closer to that image than we are, we must assume she's someone to beat. But this is silly, of course, and nothing more than perception. There is no ideal; it's all fabricated. We are all going after different things but find ourselves sometimes steering into the false ideal that society (and *Vogue*!) has set before us.

When I first met Melissa, I didn't stop to think that perhaps she just had a different way of coping with her struggles as a new mom (which I found out years later was true). Or that perhaps the only reason she was holding her son that night was because they came late and didn't know childcare was available (I found out later this was also true). Or that maybe, just *maybe*, I intimidated her as well (also true).

Instead, I saw her as an opponent.

I looked at her and assumed I was witnessing a woman being *better* than I was. Handling motherhood better. Bonding to her child quicker. Balancing work more easily. Losing the pregnancy weight faster.

Which leads me to the other aspect of womanhood that exhausts me: salads as a meal. When did this become standard practice for women? I'm not saying a salad with a whole chicken breast on it mixed with avocados, cheese, eggs, and tortilla chips smothered in twelve ounces of ranch dressing can't be a meal. But ordering a small side salad—without croutons and with the dressing on the side—and telling me that "it just sounds good" is the practice of the clinically insane. Or a crazy ritual of competitors. Mind games. Trash talk.

The only thing worse than watching a beautiful, brilliant friend pick at a small plate of grass is hearing the abuse she heaps on herself while she does it, claiming she needed to eat a salad for lunch because she "had a carby breakfast" or because she's "been so bad lately."

I have no issues with wanting to be healthy. I make—for the most part—healthy choices in my day-to-day life. I cook myself a healthy and intricate breakfast every morning. I cook most nights of the week. I frequently purchase almonds and make substantial efforts to eat them. I drink about ninety ounces of water a day. I can't tell you the last time I had a candy bar. And, given enough nacho cheese sauce, I can really wolf down some vegetables.

My issue is how women punish themselves for every crumb that hits their lips. Or the sweeping declarations they make, like if they eat carbs they just "balloon up." Or the bold lifestyle choices they constantly take on, like giving up sugar or only eating "clean." And what the hell is with all the juice cleanses? Here, take this spinach, mush it up, drink it, and shit constantly for a week. You'll feel amazing!

I can't help but think the only reason any woman would subject herself to that torture is because she's trying to achieve a standard put on her by someone else, to become a worthy opponent. She sees a healthier, skinnier, firmer woman and goes into juice-cleanse, shitting-round-the-clock, salad-as-a-meal, hyper-competitive mode. So then there's a beautiful, talented, brilliant woman who spends way too much time obsessing over food and weight and gluten. Using food as a punishment.

Self-loathing. Feeling guilt while eating. And nothing ruins a good steak like tears.

Again, making good choices is fine: drinking water instead of Coke, fruit as a side, less red meat, move your body more. Many, many people do this without even giving it a thought, or attaching it to a childhood memory, or posting about it on Facebook.

These people are called men.

Men don't sit around picking shamefully at their food, nor do they sit around comparing themselves to other men. My husband has never once looked at another man and said, "Do you think he's a better father than I am?" Nor has he taken so much as a breath while inhaling bacon.

Without constantly being threatened by one another, and without giving a thought to eating sugar or enjoying a stiff drink, men have all the time in the world to walk around inventing shit and getting paid twice as much for it.

I'm fully aware of the pressures on women that their male counterparts don't experience. I think the 2016 election cycle proved that. But maybe, just *maybe*, if we women all started acting like that pressure wasn't there, it might one day disappear. If we started looking at each other as teammates before opponents, then we could stop all the competition and take one another out for lunch.

And order a hamburger.

We would stop picking at our food. We would stop comparing ourselves to other women. We would stop thinking that spin class is the only reason we're allowed to eat a bite of cake. And we could put our energy more on taking down the man. We can start by eating some fries off his plate.

I speak from experience. Three years after that first dinner where I met Melissa, she and I became close friends. It started because our children are friends. Her son Jack and my daughter Lowery adore each other in a beautiful, simple way that children can before the expectations of society are thrust upon them.

When Melissa and I became pregnant at the same time with our second children, we formed a deeper bond. Text messages, emails, and meals together helped us move past the competition and into a place that felt nurturing and comfortable.

When our second children were born—both little girls—we celebrated their health and were each grateful for our body's ability to carry them. We don't talk about breastfeeding, losing baby weight, or our favorite low-fat Crock-Pot recipes. And when we want to share a meal, we don't raise the stakes by ordering a salad.

Now, my younger daughter, London, and Melissa's daughter, Katy, are in daycare class together. On London's first day, I was emotional. At work, I sat at my desk crying and scrolling through the pictures of her birth while R.E.M. played in the background. Then my phone lit up with a text from Melissa. It was a picture she had snapped of our daughters. During drop-off, she had laid Katy down beside London on a big mat in the classroom. Instinctively, the girls had extended their arms and grasped each other's hands. It was only for a moment, Melissa explained, but it was a palpable love between two female friends.

So perhaps the next generation of women won't have this cyclical competition problem. Maybe those women will have it all figured out. They'll spend time talking about improving lives and changing the world and saving the planet. And they won't get hung up on the next diet or exercise fad or boast about their parenting philosophies all over social media.

Maybe the women of the next generation will just be who they are and be proud of it. They will figure out early on that they are equal to the opposite gender, the way Lowery and Jack did. And maybe they will discover early on that they are equal to one another, the way London and Katy have.

They won't compete. And they will eat. This is the hope I have for the next generation of women because this is who I'm helping to raise. Here's my driving thought every day as I do: I peek into the future, twenty years down the road, and I see my daughters at lunch together. They meet regularly because they are close, best friends even. It catches my breath how beautiful and strong they've become. They laugh while eating their sandwiches. And while I can't quite make out what they are saying, I hope they are discussing their greatest passions in life and relishing in each other's different ambitions. I want them to understand that competition doesn't exist between the two of them; it never did. And that it doesn't exist between anyone else either. I hope they are remembering to ignore the wants of others and focus on their own desires, and that they are encouraging each other. Above all, I just hope they are talking about something of substance. But not of weight.

DON'T CONTROL THE WANTS OF OTHERS, AND DON'T LET THE WANTS OF OTHERS CONTROL YOU

Once you've stopped confusing your wants with the wants of others, it's hard not to try to make others want what *you* want. Especially when it comes to controlling the remote on a Friday night. One of the harder life lessons to learn is standing your ground when you feel shaky. This means accepting the choices you've made and the life you want even if they don't look anything like anyone else's. It especially means not trying to convince others they should walk your path (*cough*, CrossFit, *cough*). Choosing the life you want is overwhelming, even if it involves simple decisions like what to feed your kids or what kind of car to buy. So to validate those choices you may feel the need to convince others to join in.

On the eve of our college graduation, my roommate and I got into a terrible fight. Like, a screaming in a parking lot at full volume kind of fight. The fight was over what we were going to do after graduation. She wanted to move as far away from her hometown as possible, maybe even to a different country. I wanted to move back closer to home. For whatever reason, this difference made us constantly erupt into fights. Finally, that night in the parking lot, she screamed at me, "Why does it make you so damn mad that I want to move far away?!" To which, in a moment of vulnerability and anger, I yelled, "Because it makes me feel like a loser for wanting to move back home!" She stopped and looked at me and then started laughing. "How does my decision make your decision a bad one?" I had been stewing about her life decision because I was clearly feeling insecure about my own.

Conformity is a very real thing, and while it isn't always bad (who doesn't love cheering for their favorite sports team or Real Housewife?), it can come at the expense of following your own path. As far back as the 1950s, researchers Deutsch and Gerard looked at what influences our behaviors. They posited there were two types of conformity motivation. The first is that people seek conformity to justify their interpretation of reality and, essentially, behave correctly. At least following the rules lets us know we are doing something right. The second is that people are motivated to conform as a means to seek approval from others. You know, smoking in the girls' room. Now think about those two motivations. At their root is an idea of belonging. We may have strong desires in our life, but if they don't match up with the dreams of others (and they shouldn't!), we might start to feel alone.

As you strive for your biggest goals, you will enter what I call the *crazy straw continuum*, based on its cyclical though inclining trajectory. Here's how it goes: People make the boldest choices when they are feeling the most stable. Stability is a springboard for risk-taking. But people will shy away from career opportunities if, say, their personal lives are a mess. Instability is an impediment to innovation. We have to find our balance before we can choose to do something that might throw it back out again. So we put a lot of energy into feeling stable, and we feel most stable when we belong to something: a group of friends, a good neighborhood, a team at work, a professional association, or a graduate program. When you have a sense of belonging, you use that stability to go out and do something bold—start a new career, a new diet, a new relationship. Yet once you do strike out on your own, you may suddenly find yourself a little scared and perhaps a little alone. So you might do the next logical thing: convince others to have your same dreams. Join the same company! Start this diet with me! Let's both date this new guy!

The continuum repeats itself over and over. This process is inevitable, but it's also great because it isn't just a continual circle leading to nowhere; it's a loopy incline—a crazy straw—headed upward. You will seek stability through belonging and only then can you move ahead. Once you do, you will clamor for stability and belonging. Revel in being part of a cycle that propels you forward. New students in the program are always cautious to start graduate school, often intimidated by their classmates or concerned about their own intellect and ability. A semester later they feel calmer and more stable, and that's typically when they come to my office asking whether I know of any new job opportunities.

Standing your ground means letting go of the belonging and feeling stable, so you can stretch a bit. If you keep your own goals in mind and trust in yourself, you will get exactly where you need to go—around and up through the crazy straw.

Now, while you have to be understanding of the fact that not everyone is going to play life by your rules—they may not have the same motivations or work as hard or for the same rewards—you must also accept that other people need to be understanding of you. That's right. You have to let others go so they will let you go.

Whether on purpose or subconsciously out of their own insecurity, others will try to interfere with the choices you've made. In fact, findings from the 1955 study by Deustch and Gerard still hold true more than sixty years later—there are two motivations for why we seek conformity: you are either validating your own choices to believe you're living right, or you are seeking the approval of others. But the studies that followed Deutsch and Gerard's, particularly from David and Turner in 2001, drew an important conclusion: While those two motivations are in fact independent of each other, they are also incredibly difficult to disentangle. We can't tell which motivation is stronger, which comes first, or which is easier to get over. This means you might find yourself in a crazy straw continuum—going back and forth between wanting to conform and wanting to break away. Recognize this cycle will lead you to higher ground if you let it. Just like in a crazy straw, if there's no force propelling it, the chocolate milk just stays in the crook of a loop. Let go of others' wants, let them let go of yours, and propel yourself upward.

• • •

Recently, a crew from the city where I live was patching some asphalt on our street when I came home from work. As I got out of my car, one of the crewmen approached me to ask whether he could take a picture of the sycamore in our backyard. This tree sits close to our house, just outside the living room window. Its trunk is so massive that it would take three men standing around it touching fingertips to mimic its circumference. The tree is so tall it shoots out and over the top of our two-story home, nearly fifty feet above the tallest peak of the roof. The branches jut out in all directions, with limbs the size of most average trees, and the leaves that cloak it are larger than an adult face.

This tree was one of the major selling features of the home. When my husband and I first pulled up to the house and saw the massive tree brilliantly shading the sweet home below it, we gasped. "I know," our realtor beamed. "I know."

We've now officially seen the tree through every Oklahoma season. In the heat of the summer, we benefited greatly from the behemoth and all its widespread and lustrous foliage. The shade kept the backyard cool and our cooling bill low. As we rolled into autumn, we were impressed, if not amused, at how many leaves fell from our great tree. Leaf after leaf after leaf piled up and blocked our front door, covering our driveway and clogging our gutters. We had to call in professionals. After a month or so, the leaves were all gone and we saw our beautiful sycamore naked for the first time. With the tree bare, its healthy, robust, and gothic outline was breathtaking against the clear blue sky. When we endured our first snow and ice storm, we were awakened in the middle of the night by enormous, frozen branches snapping and hitting the roof.

Over the years we've watched the tree grow and change with the seasons. It has provided us shelter, shade, atmosphere, and beauty. I'm enamored of our home, our street, and our neighbors. But the tree? It's my greatest point of pride. Yet despite my pride and confidence in the gorgeous, giant creature that frames our home, I'm not without my doubts that it's always beneficial to our family.

Once, while pregnant with London, and with my husband in Singapore on business, I was home alone with then two-and-a-half-year-old Lowery in the middle of a tornado. I heard the wind howl as I made my way up-stairs to bed. I turned on the TV to see if this was a storm that should have me fleeing to our basement for shelter. The meteorologist explained that a tornado was moving toward us and to expect to take caution and cover until morning.

I heard a thump. I peered outside to see our trash can swirling around in the air, beating against the side of the house and slamming into the fence. I ran upstairs, the wind getting stronger with every step I took. I threw open the curtains in my sleeping child's room to see trees in our neighbors' yard leaning over in the forceful winds. I looked up to see the sycamore branches reaching out over the roofline like giant skeleton hands. In that moment, I was terrified of our big, beautiful tree.

Without hesitating, I reached for my child and ran down two flights of stairs and into our basement. Low-ery curled up next to me—contouring herself around my pregnant belly—foggy with sleep. We lay together on the couch, wrapped tightly. I held her close, studying her beautiful sleeping face as I heard what sounded like more objects in our backyard being hoisted up and thrown about. I tried to decipher each noise. Glass breaking? Patio furniture catapulting? Shingles ripping from the roof? But as I lay there, embracing my precious child, I was worried about only one thing: our sycamore. I feared that it would be uprooted and would come crashing down on our house. Never in my life, not ever so much as in that moment, did I feel more like a mother.

While I've read numerous articles on the care of sycamore trees, I don't turn to parenting books. I've become so beaten down by articles people write or links friends share that I've given up reading almost everything on the topic. I take such pride in my mighty children—their intellect, personalities, and twinkly eyes. I use my children as the only yardstick to measure how good I am as a mother. They are incredibly bonded to me, loving, happy, healthy, and smart. And so, rightly or wrongly, I've taken their thriving as a sign I must be doing something right.

A couple of weeks before the storm, a good friend and I had an intense debate about where we plan to send our children to school. The public/private school debate is as irritating and pointless as the breastfeeding/formula debate, but I've accepted that there's a debate at every stage.

My friend—whom I consider to be a wonderful mother—and I became entangled in a heated conversation about the benefits of private school versus public school, and her assertion that if she were to make the wrong choice, her children would suffer and forever be at a disadvantage.

I posited that while choosing a school is a personal and difficult choice, it will not necessarily ruin a child's life or be anywhere near the only decision that will set them up for failure or success. I argued that while choosing a school is important and I, too, struggle with the decision, I believe a child's education comes from many sources.

After our debate, I found myself upset for reasons I couldn't comprehend. She and I had engaged in lively debates a dozen times before without so much as a blink. After days of stewing over my unexplained emotions, I realized that what was bothering me was that I feared my friend didn't think I was a good mother.

Perhaps she took my more relaxed approach to choosing a school as a sign I wasn't invested in my child's future. Or that the choice I was planning to make (public) wasn't a good one, as it wasn't sacrificing enough (financially) to ensure my child's success.

More specifically, I was upset that she, or any of my friends, would measure my ability as a mother only by the choices I make among those polarizing options in parenting. For all the kind things said among friends, rarely is there praise for one another's parenting. And for the first time, despite the self-confidence in my parenting that I had worked hard to build, I felt the winds of doubt blowing through the cracks.

But during the night of the storm, as I trembled in fear amid the sounds of angry wind, imagining every possible outcome with my child tucked safely under my arm, I had a revelation about motherhood. Most of my worry came from the dizzying effect of being within the crazy straw continuum. I had felt stable in my marriage and professional life when we decided to have a child. When Lowery was born, I suddenly felt alone and scared and clamored to find a community of other mothers who could help me stabilize. And while I value the comfort I gained from my friends with children, after a while I began to feel the need to branch out on my own in the role, to do things differently than they do and walk my own path as a mother. Which meant making decisions that might go against the grain. Rejecting the common practices of my peers felt scary at first, and I feared my individual choices might be wrong or bad. But I soon recognized I could find stability within my relationship to my daughter. After all, she was the only person who could judge whether I was a good mother. And she was snuggled close to me for strength and comfort.

The next morning we crawled out of our basement and opened the back door to assess the damage. I was surprised to find that everything was in its place, with the exception of the trash can, which had landed in the far corner of the yard. The patio furniture had barely moved. I must have imagined the sound of glass breaking. Only a handful of broken limbs littered our yard. And as I stepped outside and peered up at the sycamore towering above our house, I was relieved to see it was still standing, as tall and strong as ever.

Having defiantly survived the storm.

REJECTING YOUR WANTS, AND WHEN YOUR WANTS REJECT YOU

The thing about wants is, they change. You change your mind about what you want for a million reasons. And sometimes the wants we have reject us—like an organ transplant that just will not attach.

A study out of Uppsala University in Sweden looked at a large group of aspiring fiction writers to create a framework for understanding the turmoil that comes from trying to succeed at something with such a high rate of failure. Sometimes writers simply realized they don't want to be writers (they get to do the rejecting), sometimes they felt they could never get published (others do the rejecting), and sometimes they were most concerned about what others would think about them for failing (their peers reject them). The researchers wanted to look at these three potential outcomes for pursuing a dream. Essentially, at every step along the way of going after what they wanted, these writers were both hopeful and fearful. They were not giving a damn what anyone thought, and simultaneously worried about how others would perceive their rejection. In the end, the researchers found four ways of coping with rejection: 1) conceding; "I guess I'm just not the writer I thought I was." 2) excusing; "Writing is so difficult anyway—most writers struggle their whole lives and their careers never amount to anything." 3) justifying; "Working a full-time job and raising kids is why I haven't gotten further along in my writing." 4) refusing; "This rejection letter doesn't mean anything. I just need to find a better publication more in line with my writing style." Two of these behaviors—conceding and justifying—show a sense of responsibility for the failure. But in the end, the researchers noted that those writers who showed the most resilience did two things: claim responsibility, but not see rejection as failure.

You see, rejection is coming your way. It already has. Sometimes you get rejected—you didn't get the job, your spouse left you, you didn't get accepted to law school. And sometimes you do the rejecting—you turned down the job, you left your spouse, you decided you didn't even want to apply to law school. The point of life isn't to avoid rejection; it's to accept it (try and understand it) and learn from it.

• • •

During my senior year of high school, my parents told me they would happily take me to tour any colleges in which I might have an interest. So I asked them to drive me ten hours to a little town three states away. The college is renowned for its creative writing program, award-winning library, and high national ranking in overall pretentiousness.

We loaded up my parents' Suburban and drove north until we hit snow. When we arrived on campus, we were greeted by a tall, skinny junior with long, dirty hair, wearing shorts, flip flops, and a hoodie that read, "Privatize This" with a picture of a brain on it. With the straightest of expressions, he introduced himself as "Pear." I was irked when my father chuckled. Even more so when he said, "I'm sorry, Perry is it?"

"No," said Pear. "It's *Pear*. Like the fruit."

Pear took us around the campus and showed us the art studios, the writing labs, the expressive yoga rooms, the reading lofts, and the cafeteria that served mostly vegan foods. When he walked us across the quad he took his shoes off so his "toes could be one with the grass." We passed a couple making out on a hemp blanket and a guitar-playing loner who was, according to Pear, the poetry department chair.

After our campus tour, I was scheduled to be interviewed by the dean of admissions, who had reviewed my application and was "decently impressed" with my entrance essay but thought meeting me would help the committee make its final decision. I left my parents with Pear to—as I can only assume—smoke a bowl, and went into my two-hour interview.

Many of the questions were well above my knowledge base, but I was able to give her honest and robust reflections on the latest Jonathan Franzen novel, and I nailed the question about the nation's abuse of the semicolon. I walked away knowing that, while I may not have been perfect, I had done the best I could.

When we left campus, Pear waving to us in the rearview mirror, I knew one thing: I wanted to be accepted. And so, back at home, I waited. And waited. Until one day, months after our visit, I received a very flat envelope with the college's logo in the top left corner. They regretted to inform me, but they did not think I was a good fit for their program.

No nationally renowned writing program. No award-winning library. No making out with Pear, wearing ponchos, while our friends played hacky sack to the music our poetry professor belted out across the quad. I had been rejected. My father was uncomfortable with my sadness. He wanted nothing more than to move past this misfortune and continue on with more campus tours.

My mother, on the other hand, was vengeful. She took the letter, pressed it out flat, and read it over and over and over. Then she opened the file folder in which she kept only the most important of documents, which included all her children's birth certificates and her tomato torte recipe, and lay the letter on top.

"Mom, why are you keeping that?" I asked through tears.

"For when you make it big, darling. I can give this to Oprah."

Yes, my mother kept that rejection letter so that Oprah would one day sit next to me on her sparkling white couch, hold my hand, and say, "I cannot believe *you*, a person beloved by *millions*, the richest, most successful woman in all the world, was once rejected by a small, liberal arts college in a cornfield! I *just* can't believe it!" And this would inevitably spark a boycott of the college, as fervent as the beef boycott she sparked in the 1990s, which would ultimately force the institution to close due to its wild unpopularity spurred by universal loyalty to me.

Later, when I settled on another college with a strong writing program, my professors encouraged me to submit my writings for publication. I sent out numerous essays to various literary journals and magazines all over the nation. I received twenty-two rejection letters all saying the same thing: No thanks.

Rejection wasn't just confined to my writing aspirations. I once professed (mentioned in passing) my deep love (moderate appreciation) for a guy I met at college who responded by saying, "You're nice, but I'm looking for someone more domestically minded to settle down with."

I was rejected by as many PhD programs as accepted me. I produced about a year's worth of negative pregnancy tests and endured a failed round of fertility treatments before I became pregnant. And during my post-doctorate job search, I was rejected left and right.

But most recently, the rejection I'm struggling with is of a more personal nature. It's the push and pull as a mother of daughters. When they seek out their father for comfort, instead of me, I respond in an irrational way. Recently, both of my daughters fell off the swing set in our backyard. Lowery scraped her knees pretty badly and London hit her head hard enough to cause a large bump to immediately protrude.

Jim and I rushed to their sides, but both daughters immediately reached for him. I tried to join in the hug, desperate to offer my love and support, but each shook me off. London slapped at me to go away while Lowery buried her face in Jim's chest. I was not what they wanted.

They wanted their father. While I should have only been concerned with their minor injuries, I felt completely hurt by their rejection. Which was, by all accounts, as ridiculous as it was selfish.

My reaction flew in the face of the pride I have in my daughters' extreme independence. I love how they spring from my arms at school drop-off while other children claw at their parents' necks, screaming dramatically. I revel in the fact that my children are self-possessed, confident, strong-willed, and wildly independent. But in that moment, when they rejected my love, I started crying alongside my hurting children, who wouldn't let me make it better.

It was momentary. After a few minutes, we were back inside. London sat beside me on the couch brushing my hair while Lowery pretended to put makeup on my face. But I couldn't shake the feeling that in a moment when my children needed someone, they didn't choose me. Even though I know it isn't personal, and I know their father brings them a tremendous amount of comfort, it made me all the more aware of how my desire for a healthy mother/daughter relationship grows stronger with each passing day. I know too many women who struggle in their relationships with their mothers. And though it's irrational to assume that what happened at the swing set is an indication of our future relationship—or even of our current relationship—I live with trepidation of ever being truly rejected one day by my girls.

There's really nothing that makes rejection sting less. It's a rotten thing to be told you aren't the right person, or you don't qualify, or you weren't a good fit, or you aren't the one, or you didn't try hard enough. Because the moment you decide to pursue something—college, a job, parenthood—you imagine yourself in the desired outcome. You picture your new dorm room, office, or growing belly, and you start to believe it's already true. So when the news comes that your desires won't be met and your dreams won't come to fruition, it's hard not to grieve the loss of the life you thought you would have. That's the worst part of it: You have no control. All you can really do is accept the rejection, even if you do it in irrational ways.

Like how my mother has held on to my rejection letter all these years. It's still there, yellowing in a folder, waiting for me to make it something of extreme irony. I realize now that she wasn't really doing that for me, though I think she still believes I can somehow stick it to the college through Oprah. She was doing it for herself as a mother. She was trying to do something for her hurting daughter when nothing could really be done. Which assures me that despite all the rejection I might endure in this lifetime, there's one acceptable upside: at least someone is keeping my information on file.

YOUR FUTURE WANTS DON'T HAVE TO JUSTIFY YOUR PAST ONES

Even if we were somehow rejected on our quest for something—or even if we reject our own previous quest for something—we can't get stuck in the past. It's easy to want things to progress in a logical way. C has to follow B, which follows A. Our whole world is set up to agree with that linear progress. Which means many people often feel that where they are currently going must validate where they have been.

When Alex came to talk to me, it was about going up for a promotion in her line of work. She was more than qualified in the field (nonprofit fundraising) and was excited to move forward in her career. But as we talked, I kept feeling a sense of hesitation from her about the opportunity. At first, I thought she was questioning her ability to move into a more visible role with more responsibility. But as we talked, I realized her issue wasn't confidence; it was doubt. As she spoke, it became clear that although she was excited to progress in her career, this was not a role she was remotely excited about. When I asked why she was even going after it, she said, "I've been in nonprofit development for five years. This is the logical next step in my career."

Well, that kind of depends on your definition of logic. You see, Alex wasn't the first person I've had in my office trying to justify their past with their future. So many prospective students come to see me and say something along the lines of, "My undergraduate degree is in an entirely different field from the job I'm currently doing, so I need a graduate degree in the field I'm in now." To which I always respond, "If that were true, you wouldn't have your job now." Not a great recruitment strategy, I realize. See, if we start down a path after something we wanted in our past, we often use that as an excuse to keep going down that same path, even when our wants have changed.

This is what researchers call *status quo bias,* the idea that humans favor familiarity when making a decision. Status quo bias pops up in all kinds of research, in everything from how people make political choices in the voting booth to how they decide which house to buy. Researchers Kahenman and Tyversky concluded that the loss of something is twice as psychologically harmful as the gains would be beneficial. You would feel twice as much pain from losing $1,000 as you would get pleasure from gaining $1,000. We are far more protective of what we have than excited by what we want.

This concept plays out a lot when students think about changing careers. The new line of work might offer more money, but that incentive usually isn't enough to change jobs. People need to be assured there's going to be *twice* as much to gain as there is to lose by switching career paths. Many of my prospective students are considering the degree because they want to change careers, so our conversation involves them grilling me about the viability of a career in the field. They are attempting to measure whether what they are about to gain (this new career path) is going to far outpace what they are giving up (old career). They are usually frustrated by some key element of their current career (too corporate, no flexibility, can't move up, not passionate about it), but they still want to weigh whether a new career will counterbalance that key element *and* offer the things about their current job they do like (good coworkers, decent commute, low stress, quality coffee in the break room). We cling to what we have—even when we are clearly uninspired by it—far more tightly than we cling to what *could be*. Essentially, you won't change the status quo unless you believe with certainty that the gains will be at least twice as much as the potential loss. And when it comes to making life decisions—like changing careers, moving, or divorce— that's a certainty we can't ever truly predict. So we stick to the status quo.

Alex was concerned her time as a fundraiser would be wasted if she didn't use all her skills in the job at the top of that field. But luckily, Alex decided to be okay with going out on a limb with brand-new wants—utilizing her experience from pursuing past wants—and was offered a nice job in a corporation as head of business develop- ment. Wants change, but skills transfer, and all experience is experience. Don't keep going down a path just because you're already on it. It's still progress to change directions, especially if it gets you to where you'd rather go. I always find my true wants at the corner of my past and present self.

• • •

One summer, my childhood friend Elizabeth got married on her parents' land in our hometown. Given the nature of our small town, most everyone from our past was set to come. And sometimes facing your past is difficult. Even with two layers of Spanx.

Elizabeth is a world traveler, if not, perhaps, a pro- fessional nomad. She's lived and traveled all over and has picked up numerous interesting and dynamic friends along the way.

Her wedding was much like an international airport, with strangers from around the world uniting for a common purpose. Her friends from her life in Washington, D.C., from her many travels, her time in law school, camp and college, and, of course, our hometown were there.

It quickly became evident there was a divide among Elizabeth's friends: Everyone after high school knows her only as *Liz*. Upon meeting all of her new friends, they would ask how I knew Liz. I would say that I didn't know Liz, but I knew *Elizabeth* quite well. When I used her full name, they would say, "Oh, you must have gone to high school together." But in our town, saying you "went to high school together" is like saying you climbed the last three feet of Kilimanjaro's peak.

I *grew up* with Elizabeth. Our parents were best friends before we were ever born. We sold Girl Scout cookies together, were in the same dance class, had sleepovers, got our driver's licenses together, went to prom together, and met every Sunday for breakfast while she was in law school, and my mother made her wedding cake, as well as the wedding cake for her sister, who married my cousin, whom she met at my wedding.

But, yes, I suppose we did also go to high school together.

Those who know *Elizabeth* remember her as organized, smart, studious, and ambitious. Always in T-shirts, jeans, and glasses, with her hair styled in a straight, chin-length bob. Those who met *Liz* know the easygoing free spirit with the contact lenses; flawlessly chic clothing; and long, flowing, wavy hair.

The wedding weekend was a festival of events: a bachelorette party, rehearsal and rehearsal dinner, post-rehearsal dinner party, bonfire, bridal brunch, professional photo shoot, wedding, reception, photo booth, lighting of the wish lanterns, and the post-wedding hangover.

These events provided ample time to meet new people, most of whom didn't personally know of Elizabeth's past in our hometown. Which meant they also didn't know of mine. They were meeting the Meg who was a married mother with a career. They didn't know of the Past Meg, who was once inexplicably into reggae music and wore a lot of tie-dye. And this is what is so exhilarating about meeting new people: a fresh start every time. Introduce yourself with control of the information. But you can't ignore your past because it always shows up to weddings.

After the rehearsal dinner, guests were treated to a slideshow presentation in which we watched Elizabeth evolve into Liz. One picture caught me by surprise: a picture of Elizabeth and me at graduation, in our caps and gowns, clutching our diplomas while hugging each other around the neck. Elizabeth's eyes were glassy, puffy, and red. Mine were bright and happy. I turned to my good friend Lindsey and asked whether she had cried at our high school graduation. She leaned in and whispered, "I think you were the only one who didn't."

There I was, in the picture, unmoved by the thought of leaving high school. Meanwhile, my classmates around me, the people I'd grown up with, seemed like this was a tragic end to something. It was only in that moment, ten years later, married with a child, that I felt a pang for my past.

During the bridal brunch the next day, one of Liz's friends asked what I was like in high school. One of Elizabeth's friends interjected before I could speak: "Meg was the same then as she is now!"

Especially my hair.

The fall semester began the next week. I was still teaching as an adjunct to undergraduates. I walked into my upper-level-division ethics class and scanned the room. Some students I had seen before in the hallways; others I knew by reputation. A few had been in my class the previous semester. Mostly, as I prefer it, there was a room full of fresh new faces staring back at me. But after introductions and once I started the lecture, the door flew open and in walked a familiar face: a girl named Tracy. I remembered her from the first course I ever taught.

When she was originally in my class, four years earlier, she was impossibly thin, had dark hair streaked with bleach, and wore braces on her teeth. Back then she sat in the front row, wore pathetically short shorts and low-cut tops, and smacked her gum throughout my lectures. She talked a lot, too. She often blurted out thoughtless comments that brought on muffled laughter from the rows behind her. And while I typically defend everyone's opinion in my class, even I shuddered when she announced one day that she would never have children because she didn't want to "lose her body."

"Remember me?" she asked as she took a seat near the back.

Of course I did. Except I noticed she had filled out just slightly, giving her a healthy glow. She was wearing a nice dress of appropriate length. Her hair was a natural color, and her braces were gone. She looked so much older to me in that moment that I wondered what she thought of my appearance and whether I looked different to her.

Except for my hair.

I prepared myself for her childish comments during my lecture. I prepared myself to have to break up her whispering to a friend during class. I was even prepared to stay after class every week to help her further with the material.

But then a funny thing happened. She listened attentively to my lecture, took notes, and raised her hand to interject a comment while the class discussed the ethical dilemma of politicians who get caught sexting. She spoke with confidence and made a compelling argument for the problems of political figures losing public trust. And she didn't laugh once when she said "Anthony Weiner."

Even I couldn't manage that.

After class she came up and gave me a hug. She said she was thrilled to see me again and that she had heard from others who had taken my classes that I had finished my PhD and had a baby since I last saw her. She mentioned that she herself had gotten married, becoming a stepmother in the process, and had been given a promotion at work, which prompted her to finally declare a major. Standing in front of me was a poised and beautiful woman. She asked a few questions about the upcoming assignment, thanked me for my time, and walked gracefully out of the classroom.

Moments later she poked her head back in and said, "Oh! *Weiner*. Like a man's wiener! I just now got that! Hilarious!" That moment reminded me of the car ride home from Elizabeth's wedding. I told my husband that meeting all of Elizabeth's new friends was a relief. When he asked why, I explained that I was worried she had changed too much, or that the Elizabeth I knew was gone, replaced by Liz. But in meeting Liz's friends, it was obvious that she, at her core, was the same good person she's always been.

Then I recounted all the many great conversations I had with my former high school classmates, some of whom I hadn't seen in years. And I began to cry.

"What's wrong?" he asked. "Why are you crying?"

"I guess I just miss them," I shrugged. "In a different way than I did when we graduated."

Which made me feel a bit better, because the only thing worse than people from your past thinking you are nothing like they remember you is having them think:

You haven't changed a bit.

YOUR WANTS HAVE A TIMELINE, NOT A DEADLINE

It may take some time to sift through all the confusion and separate your wants from everyone else's. But when you finally figure it out and are secure enough in your wants not to project them onto others (or let others project theirs onto you), you'll be faced with another looming concern: *when*. When should you have the career, the spouse, the kids, the closet from *Clueless*? Women like timelines and deadlines. Our tampons are measured by the hour, and we demanded our yeast infection treatments be reduced from a full week to a lunch hour.

Many of my students are visibly stressed about their timelines. I get a lot of hand-wringing in my office. They have to get going on everything, right now, all the time; they are already behind! But again, if you aren't getting your wants confused with the wants of others, you shouldn't have a timeline based on anything but your own feasibility.

Recently, a student of mine, Margret, was talking to me about her career path. She was a development director at a small nonprofit. I suggested she apply for the executive director position that had just opened up at a major organization. She batted her hand at me and said, "It's not time." I looked at her quizzically, so she explained, "I've only been in my current job for five months." When I reminded her she had years of experience before that, she pushed back: "I need to stay somewhere for at least a year before making another move or it will look like I can't commit." I shrugged. She kept going. "I need exactly two more years of development experience and then I'd like to get at least a year of financial management training." I shrugged again. When she was done listing all the reasons she couldn't apply for a job I knew she'd be great at, I looked at her and said, "But the job is available *right now*. Screw your timelines." So she applied, went through an intensive six-month hiring process, and was selected as the best candidate.

Now, plenty of stuff could have happened along the way. She could have been eliminated for lack of experience (she brought the most of all the candidates). She could have decided she didn't want the role after all (over the six-month interview process she became enamored of the position). Or she could have stuck to her original timeline only to come out the other side either without the same opportunity available or perhaps wanting an entirely different career (I've seen both happen with other students).

We put arbitrary deadlines on things that don't actually have deadlines. We think all hiring managers are looking for *exactly* seven years of experience. Or we think we won't be ready for something until we have a bit more education. But opportunities come when they come and we are usually more than ready for them, whether we know it or not. That's especially true when it comes to deciding when to have children.

According to the Centers for Disease Control, the average age of first-time moms has increased by 3.3 years—from 22.7 to 26 years—since 1980. That may not seem like a big shift in 40 years, but think about what that means. The timeline is changing. Women will still set arbitrary deadlines on their life—married by 30! Babies by 35! Nobel by 40! But as a whole, women (at least American women) are pushing that timeline further and further back. Which means even something as overwhelming as when to have kids doesn't have a deadline. It is a moving target.

Many of my graduate students are contemplating when to have children. They come to my office expecting me to have the perfect answer. I'll close my eyes, tap into their aura, and then calmly whisper, "At thirty-two years of age." They will nod serenely and off they'll go, knowing when the right time is.

Ironically, education and baby-making have been historically intertwined among the female sex. As economist Heinrich Hock explained in his 2005 paper, one of the leading indicators in a woman's ability to obtain a college degree is her access to contraceptives. Now, granted, this points to a systemic issue of socioeconomic status and the educational divide, but just think about that for a minute. Back when birth control came on the scene, there was an impressive uptick in the number of women obtaining college degrees. And since the 1980s, higher education across the US has shifted to being female-dominated. Fast forward to now. I run a graduate program that is comprised of 65 percent women, and a majority of those are in my office saying, "Wait, *when* do I bring in a baby?"

There's a historical, societal, and perhaps internal tension that women can't pursue babies and education simultaneously. So there starts our timeline. Baby first, then school! School first, then baby! While there are other factors to consider—cost, time, does Lisa Frank make Trapper Keepers for the adult learner?—I'd argue that women fundamentally believe there is a perfect time for everything and that all those perfect times are mutually exclusive. Most of the female prospective students I speak to mention their desire for babies, or their current family structure, within the first few minutes of our meeting, as if to warn me that coming back to school is going to be nearly impossible because of their current and/or future children. Women need to break the pattern of putting their kids between themselves and their education or other aspirations. Sometimes we do this as default. Sometimes we do it as armor.

But taking things when they come instead of waiting for the right time can lead to unexpected and positive outcomes. Friends, family, and colleagues told me to wait until after I finished my doctorate to start having kids. Not a single man I went to college with was told this, by the way. But I was led to believe there was a time for school and a time for babies. Yet I was excited about starting a family *and* graduate school, so I did both at the same time. This wasn't easy at first (and I discuss this in depth later), but it ultimately had unexpected and positive outcomes. You see, it forced my husband and me to share duties, guilt, and stress around parenting equally. Though my husband was already primed to be a solid and equal contributor, I believe we would have been more likely to succumb to stereotypical gender roles in parenting if it weren't for the grueling demands of my schooling. We had no choice but to be equal and to give equally. Perhaps if I had had kids first, I would have kept delaying school because our roles would have looked different and I may have felt more of the parental responsibility. When I graduated with my PhD I had one child and another on the way. By that time, we had established a rhythm and expectation around our shared parenting. So when career opportunities started to crop up it was much easier for me to feel good about taking them because I had a strong family dynamic already in place. Goes to show that the right time isn't given; it's taken.

It's okay to have an idea of when you might want something. But more often than not, opportunities arise at moments that won't align with your timeline. Sometimes it seems as if everything comes at once or not at all. Don't get too wrapped up in the *when* because it all happens exactly when it should. And it's always too fast.

• • •

My doctor came strolling into the hospital room—with me in bed feeding our newborn daughter—and shook my husband's hand in congratulations.

"So," he said as he took a seat in the room's rocking chair. "Let's talk birth control."

I let out a snort as my husband looked at him in disbelief.

"Oh," he said smiling as he waved a hand. "I don't mean for use today, obviously."

"Well," I said, inhaling greatly as I looked at our baby, "this is our last one."

"Enough already, huh?" He turned to my husband. "Okay, so are we making this permanent?"

"Yes," Jim replied. "Anyone you would recommend to do the procedure?"

The doctor took out a small note pad and quickly wrote down a few names and numbers. He told us most vasectomies book out about six months in advance, so it would be in our best interest to call as soon as possible. Not only that, but after the procedure was done, it would take a while for it to become effective.

"About thirty ejaculations before the vasectomy actually takes," he said.

"Okay, so like a month," I stated. He raised his eyebrows and looked at Jim.

"Oh!" My face began to feel hot. "I thought you meant days! Thirty days!" I stammered.

"Trust me, thirty ejaculations would *not* be a month." The doctor let out a chuckle.

"I mean, it's not like it would be much longer than a month," I clarified. "Well, it just depends on our work schedules. And the kids. Or if it's sweeps week. You know how it goes when you're tired…"

"Meg, just stop," Jim interrupted, holding up his hand.

The doctor pulled out his pad again, wrote a prescription for birth control pills, and handed it to me. "Might also use condoms," he suggested. "You know," and here he clucked his tongue, "belt *and* suspenders."

A few days after returning home from the hospital with our beautiful new baby, Jim decided to call the urologist's office. Assuming it would take months to get an appointment, we were shocked to discover the urologist could see him the very next day.

I felt foolish and guilty accompanying my husband to a vasectomy consultation with a three-day-old baby. As if our next stop was the maternity ward to drop her off with a note pinned to her onesie: *Yeah, this just isn't for us. Thanks anyway!*

But when we got to the waiting room, I was surprised to see it was designed for children. Puzzles, toy cars, and building blocks were in abundant supply, and children were *everywhere*. Climbing on furniture, ripping up magazines, and pounding on the aquarium glass. If a man were wavering about whether to get a vasectomy, a urologist's waiting room would surely convince him.

I found it oddly enjoyable watching a room full of men, squeamish and red-faced, waiting for their names to be called. After two pregnancies, during which Jim sat with me in the waiting rooms watching woman after woman waddle in to endure a cervical check, pap smear, or transvaginal ultrasound, it was validating to see man after man hold his crotch protectively while trudging down the hall with the nurse.

My husband went back for the consultation by himself. I waited in the lobby, holding our darling infant child. He was back within minutes. He reported that the doctor was no-nonsense (fine with Jim) and not much of a talker (even better). He had given Jim a stack of pamphlets, a prescription for Valium, and an appointment card for a few months later. And for the first time, looking down at the card with the date written in ink, I began to have doubts.

I never really had a vision in my head of what my family would look like. I never gave much thought to what kind of person my husband would be, though I had hoped for someone nice and smart. And I never gave much thought to how many children I would have or what gender they would be. I just hoped for some who were nice and smart.

Jim, on the other hand, had all this in his head. Early in our courtship, while walking our dogs in the park, Jim—who is never shy about saying what he wants, especially on a third date—declared to me, "I would like to have two children. Girls, if possible."

In the moment, I let out something that resembled nervous laughter and slapped him on the arm playfully. But driving back to my apartment later that day, I realized it wasn't just a casual statement. Jim rarely makes any. It was a proposal—for a life he wanted to have with me.

And I realized I wanted it, too.

So it took me by surprise that after our second daughter was born—the daughter who perfectly completed the family we always wanted—I began to question our plans.

The desire to have three children, it has occurred to me, is a societal pressure. I'm not suggesting that three isn't a great—perhaps even perfect—number of children. Many couples start their families with this number in mind. But I think many couples with two children are constantly asked when they will have the third, whereas those with three children are rarely asked about number four. For some reason, three is the number of children most people assume you and your partner will, maybe even should, have.

It's no wonder that three is the magic number in people's minds: It's the American sitcom formula. Take a couple, put them in a house with a staircase, and give them three children. Perhaps it's better fodder for comedy because all personality stereotypes can be explored.

I'm not saying that television shapes how we lead our lives, but that goddamn Rachel haircut was everywhere. So there's something to be said about the way the mind receives messages on family (and hair) and how we, even unintentionally, demand that our life imitate art.

The fact that I'm the last of three children is not lost on me. My parents certainly could have stopped at two. They nearly did. Only after my brother was seven did they decide to strive for an American sitcom. But Jim and I had always agreed we wanted two children, and only two children, for a million reasons we had been over and over and over. And for us, in our lives and with our goals, it is the best decision. But I never imagined a decision that was already made would be so difficult to carry out.

So, a few months later, in a gray, rainy fog, Jim and I slowly drove to the urologist's office. I knew deep down this was the right choice, a decision we made back when we were sane, rested, less emotional, and not under the influence of a sweet, smiley newborn's alluring power. A decision we carefully considered from all angles. A decision we made together.

But as we drove through the rain, I wondered whether Jim was having doubts. He sat so quietly beside me in the car that I wondered whether, perhaps, he was finally allowing the emotion of the situation to take over all his logical plans.

We silently walked hand in hand into the building, checked in, and took a seat in the waiting room. "Meg…" Jim finally spoke.

"Yes?"

"I'm having some concerns."

"Oh Jim, it's okay! I'm struggling too. But I think what you said is right. We can do more for two than we can for three, and you are older than me and that's something to truly consider, and our career ambitions, and our desire to travel, and the fact that four fit easily in a booth and in a car, and we can afford to take them on a plane and they have each other and we aren't outnumbered and you've always wanted two girls and they are perfect—just the *best* kids—and this last pregnancy was so hard on my body, and all the stress of paying for childcare, and who would be able to watch *three* kids for any length of time, and I don't even think I could come up with another baby name if I tried, and the house only has three bedrooms, even though I know we could technically convert the basement into a master but then we'd be two floors away from the kids and I'm just not sure that's the best idea…"

"No," he interrupted. "I'm having concerns that the Valium hasn't kicked in."

Before I could respond, the nurse called his name, and he looked down sheepishly and slowly stood. As he went down the long narrow hallway, he glanced over his shoulder at me with a reassuring look that what he was about to do—and what it would mean—was the right decision.

Within twenty minutes, he came shuffling back into the waiting room, his tall, slender body slightly hunched over.

"Well?" I asked.

"You'll be pleased to know," he said, offering a weak smile, "I had my feet in stirrups the whole time."

I suppose there was never really all that much doubt in my mind about stopping at two children. I guess it was more about the difficulty of ending that phase of our lives. I'll never experience another pregnancy. I'll never decorate another nursery. I'll never give birth again. And while it was difficult to let go of those activities, I'm more excited by what's to come.

I'm just still a little surprised at how quickly we went from that day in the park with our dogs to our family being complete.

That's the thing about it. The hardest part wasn't saying, "Enough already." The hardest part was that we had reached enough. Already.

• • •

Figuring out what we want is sometimes easy. When I wake up in the morning, I just know I want Lucky Charms. But when it comes to the bigger wants in life, we can easily get distracted—and bombarded—with a lot of mixed messages. We can want things out of life just because we want them. Our wants aren't *always* confused by our social circle, society, or that one mean prom date you are still trying to stick it to. But sometimes they are. Sometimes we get caught up in thinking we want something for reasons that have nothing to do with us. You might find yourself fixated on having three kids, but you don't stop to understand *why* three. Is it an image that was placed there before you ever started to think about having kids? You might find yourself wanting to be a CEO by the time you are thirty-five. But where did that target age come from?

All I'm suggesting is to not get bogged down in competition or comparison. Allow yourself the room to explore your interests, and don't fret too much about the demands and pressures you feel around you; chances are those pressures and demands aren't as real as you think they are. But beyond that, I promise you that no one else is trying to have your exact same life. So breathe easy knowing it's all yours for the taking.

The Closer
for TACTIC ONE

- **Understand** that you are in competition with *no one*. No one else has *your* goals, *your* expectations, or the image in *your* head of *your* ideal life. It's yours and yours alone.

- **Accept** that sometimes your wants will get rejected. They may reject you or you may reject them, but rejection can put you on the path to a better place.

- **Avoid** getting confused by the wants of others.

- **Release** others from your wants.

- **Allow** your timeline to guide your life but not dictate it. Timelines are just dots along a path; deadlines are fear-inducing directives set by professors and grumpy editors at the *New York Times*.

CHOOSING

TACTIC TWO
Choose All That Apply

People often confuse wants with choices, but they are different. Wants are abstract whereas choices are concrete. Wants are dreams; choices are reality. You can want to get married, but you'll have to choose to whom. Many students I speak with want a great career, but they struggle to choose a path. This isn't uncommon. Choices often become the enemy of wants. Bringing our wants to life must come through choice. You may decide you want to be college educated, and that desire feels good and exciting. But now you must choose a college, a major, and how you're going to pay for it. Choices are where we most often get hung up. You may worry you'll make the wrong choice, or you may be afraid to make any choice for fear it will lock you into something. If you choose to major in math, is your chance at theater suddenly gone? Want is easy; choice is hard, often because people think each choice they make will reduce the number of choices they get going forward. And if choices are finite, then you could potentially waste your limited choices and still get nowhere near what you wanted. Happily, this isn't the case.

My oldest daughter has it in her mind that negotiating for a cookie in no way makes her ineligible for a popsicle later. And yet, an hour after eating the cookie—as she's negotiating for the popsicle—she's baffled when we explain to her that she already made her choice. My daughter doesn't ever think one choice eliminates another.

Some of my students believe if they take a certain job or pursue a certain degree, they have essentially made a choice that will render them ineligible for any other choices. Every single student I talk with has several interests and skills, and numerous ideas for how her career could go. There are lots of things she wants to do. Last semester a student was talking to me about her career path in the nonprofit sector, while lamenting the fact that she couldn't also be an artist in New York. When I asked, "Why can't you?" she replied, "Well, those choices just don't make sense together." She felt she had to choose one at the expense of the other.

We've had that drilled into our heads, that we must make a choice. *The* choice. Select a major. Choose a career. Pick a small dot far off on the horizon and spend your life aiming for it. My oldest would find this line of thinking ridiculous, and I tend to agree with her.

I truly love my career in academia. I get tremendous satisfaction out of teaching and advising, and the work I do as a program administrator feels important and impactful. But my path to this job wasn't a straight line headed toward a small dot. It wasn't a choice I made in the distant past. Unlike with most academics, my job wasn't even in my plan five years ago. I was an English and creative writing major in college. Now there's a choice I know some people questioned (if I had a nickel for every person who asked what I could do with an English degree, I wouldn't have needed a job after graduation). But I simply chose what interested me at the time: writing. And even though my graduate work, research, and subsequent faculty position are in an entirely different field from English, in many ways, writing *is* my career. I write for magazines and websites, I ran a blog, I compose and deliver talks to various groups around the country, and I've authored some books. In my daughter's worldview, the choice to be a professor is the cookie, and the choice to also be a writer is the popsicle. Choosing one didn't and doesn't eliminate the other.

Yet, like my students, I struggled to make sense of these two choices I was pursuing at the same time. And when my first book came out I was conflicted about how separate I should keep these endeavors. Up to that point, they had been dirty secrets from each other. But at the book launch, when I looked out in the crowd, I was surprised to see the first row filled with my female students. Unbeknownst to me, some of my students had been reading my writing all along. They had read my very candid accounts of my own life negotiations, and that is part of why they were coming to me at the university. My writing career was unintentionally fostering healthy relationships with my students. These two choices I made at different times, and for different reasons, made perfect sense together when I stopped trying to define my career by a single choice.

Choices become overwhelming when we see them defining our lives or careers. It's easy to believe that every choice you make will eliminate other options you also might have wanted, with each choice taking you further away from other wants. But one choice will not eliminate another. Actually, the more choices you make, the more you get. Choices, after all, bring you *closer* to your wants, not further away from them. It is crucial to understand that your life and career are not hanging on one substantial choice, but they are made up of countless smaller choices. Don't spend your life aimed at a bull's-eye. Spend your life sharpening your arrows. Play to your strengths, pursue your interests, and be open to the unexpected choices, and your career and life will make sense and take shape all on their own. And it will be far grander than any small dot far off on the horizon.

SOMETIMES THE CHOICE IS MADE FOR YOU

Though I teach primarily in the field of public policy and nonprofit management, I've also had the pleasure of teaching courses for other departments on campus. I occasionally teach a few research methods and policy courses for the social work department. While the perspective of a social worker differs from the students in my own department, I've learned a lot in my time instructing social work students. Namely, that everything they do—all their studies, all their motivation—come from a place of helping people who have experienced adversity. Maybe it's poverty, or abuse, or a disability. These social work students are inspiring because their entire career is essentially turning adversity into progress; they are all about moving people past their past.

I love the studies and current attention around vulnerability. Researchers in this field have started dialogue around the things we fear most. They have given us hope that even those most terrible things that happen to us can result in wonderful progress—whether a strengthening of our own resilience, or new opportunities we couldn't have imagined. Brene Brown defines vulnerability as "uncertainty, risk, and emotional exposure." Much of her work focuses on the ways in which people overcome their adversity and use their vulnerability to make themselves stronger. The research around vulnerability is as fascinating as it is slightly uncomfortable to digest (it's choosing to read about the very things you never want to happen). But the point is, shit is going to happen to you. Shit has already happened to you. And that shit show is often the birthplace of all your best options.

This happened to me with my college boyfriend. We started to grow apart before graduation, and I was ready to end it. But graduating and starting a new adult life can be scary, and I think we both felt vulnerable in a new city, hundreds of miles away from our college friends. So out of discomfort we kept going through the motions of coupledom. Then one day, he met up with me after work and said, "I think we should break up." Suddenly, I needed this man in my life. We needed to get married! Babies! Silver anniversaries! It wasn't that I suddenly realized he was the great love of my life. I was in such a vulnerable place—new city, new job, no new friends—that I was clinging to this guy even though I knew he wasn't right for me. Ultimately, we ended things in the ugly, messy way people in their early twenties do. But later I realized that a big part of why I clung to him when he tried to end it was because he was making a choice for me that I wasn't ready to make for myself. I was already vulnerable and afraid to be alone, and then *he* got to make the call, which made me feel even more powerless over my life and my choices. I was already overwhelmed by my new life, and now I had to be back on the dating scene. This was backward thinking, of course, because once he broke up with me, a world of new possibilities opened up. Without being in a crappy relationship, I could more easily focus on work and was emotionally open to new friendships. I came to realize that *not* having this relationship meant nearly any person—any future I wanted—was once again a choice. Ultimately, it didn't matter who made the choice to break up. What mattered is that it happened.

There are many instances in life when it seems like choices are made for us. In my case, I was dumped by a guy I was already over. But even when they aren't the choices we would have made, our world suddenly opens up to nearly every other choice. Let me elaborate with a vulnerable story from my past.

• • •

For a brief period in my life, I was a mascot. A kangaroo, actually. Carey the Caring Kangaroo. My first job out of college was with a well-known and respected nonprofit organization. In the 1970s, the organization developed Carey the Kangaroo as part of a program to teach children about kindness. Or reading. Or maybe it was hygiene. The details are a bit fuzzy, but during my first week on the job, management elected me to wear the suit for a big press conference, in part because I was the newest member of the team, but also because I hadn't yet learned how to avoid eye contact during meetings. Regardless, I accepted the choice that was handed to me, and a star was born.

The costume was large and bulky, with overdramatized hips and a thick, heavy tail that swung to the beat of my gait. The belly was full of what I can only describe as dirty mattress foam, and the material down the arms was akin to the hair of a mangy mutt.

The gloves were enormous and had only four fingers, which meant keeping them on while waving to adoring crowds was difficult. To counter this obstacle, I developed a distinctive Carey wave in which I stretched my arms out in front of me, parallel to the ground, and held my hands straight up with the palms out, as though I was trying to get everyone to stop in the name of love. I'd shake my hands with rapid and quick spasms; I was waxing on and waxing off.

The feet were the size and shape of clown feet, with three furry, hard balls making up the toes. Each foot slipped over my normal street shoes. But the foot bed was made of thick, inflexible plastic, which made walking with a normal heel-to-toe step impossible. I had to lift my entire leg up high, creating a ninety-degree angle, with every step. This is why Godzilla walked the way he did.

The hood of the costume was large, and the mouth served as the windshield, but my vision was impaired because Carey didn't have a particularly toothy grin. The nose aligned with the top of my head and was hollowed out. I mounted a handheld, battery-operated fan inside the nose with a wad of Velcro. The rest of the head and the bendable, floppy ears reached out and above me, allowing Carey to stand more than six and a half feet tall. I'm five-three.

There was a lot I never imagined before becoming a mascot. For starters, kids were trickier than I thought they'd be. Too young and they were scared of me; too old and they found me annoying. I also learned that I would involuntarily and unnecessarily smile for pictures.

I had beer cans thrown at me. I had my tail pulled and my belly punched. Once, a drunk college guy dry-humped me for a laugh. Hockey fans. Amiright?

Being a mascot was a culture. Or, to be more precise, a subculture, a group committed to letting the world delight in the splendor of a charismatic creature that was silently difficult to bring to life. That small group of people was the best part of being a mascot. It was an odd privilege to be among them because so few people would be willing to endure the weight of the costume, the scream of the fans, and the pelting of beer cans. It was an odd choice to become a mascot, but there was pride in it, too.

I had an event most weekends. I was either throwing out the first pitch at a minor league baseball game, dropping the puck at a hockey game, or tossing the coin at a college football game. There were ribbon cuttings, Oktoberfest, local television appearances, and charity events. I even did a fundraising walk for some incurable disease during which a guide had to accompany me so I wouldn't wander off the trail. But the most challenging event I attended was the community's annual Mascot Dodgeball Tournament, in which all area mascots participated during halftime of an arena football game. I am proud of many things I've accomplished in my life, but being the last mascot standing on the losing team is near the top of the list. I had taken a character I had no choice in becoming and made her a winner. Or, at least, a victorious loser.

This wasn't the first time I'd negotiated such a turnaround. During the summer before my junior year of high school, I underwent total hip replacement surgery to correct for injuries sustained in a car accident while vacationing with my family in New Mexico when I was eight years old.

Hip replacement surgery is typically performed on the elderly. My grandmother had one when she was eighty after falling in the bathroom. It's not completely unheard of for infants with hip dysplasia or children with juvenile arthritis or pediatric cancer, but it's extremely rare to replace a joint on a teenager.

As a result of the car accident, I broke my right femur and was in a chest-to-toe body cast for most of the fourth grade. When the cast came off, it became clear that damage had also been done to my left hip. The impact on my body—having been thrown free of the car and landing in a ditch—destroyed the hip joint, which began losing circulation and, essentially, shriveling up like a pumpkin on a porch after Halloween. This meant that, from the age of eight until the hip replacement surgery when I was fifteen, I walked with a severe limp.

Much of my formative years seemed to have taken place inside doctors' waiting rooms. Surgeon after surgeon turned me away because they either couldn't determine what was best for my hip joint at such a young age, or they were unwilling to perform the only surgery that could stop the pain and correct the limp.

My parents tirelessly researched surgery options and surgeons, even flying me to other states to meet with specialists. After seven years of consultations, research, and physical assessments, we found a highly respected specialist willing to take my case.

At the time, seven years after the accident, I was still too traumatized to even talk about the wreck or my injuries. While my classmates certainly noticed my limp, I never mentioned it. And I did everything in my power to distract from its obviousness. Although I endured more physical pain and limitations than any child should have to, I felt profoundly lucky in a sense. Choices were made for me—I couldn't play team sports, join the cheer squad, or continue with gymnastics. I had to choose other things that I might not have considered had I been more physically capable, like speech and debate, and lots and lots of reading. I certainly resented that I couldn't live the youthful life of my peers—riding horses out to a pasture to drink beer (I grew up country) or climbing the twelve-foot-tall fence at the football stadium to drink beer on the field. Though I didn't get a choice in my physical limitations, I did get a choice to focus on attributes other than my body. I never worried about being beautiful. I didn't worry about being toned. And I certainly didn't worry with athletics, which, when you come from rural Oklahoma, is all anyone cares about, so I was, in a sense, off the hook. At least that's how I chose to see it. My body felt restricted and cumbersome, and while that was a tough burden on a young kid, it steered me in the direction of more scholarly pursuits. I couldn't play on the soccer team, but I did win some writing contests and a few spelling bees. I had no choice but to look for other choices, and the biggest choice I made was to focus from the inside out.

When we settled on the surgery, the surgeon who would perform it, and the day it would occur, I was pulled out of school constantly for numerous pre-op appointments. The last one—during which I had to give a urine sample—was during my first real period. Therefore, my transition into womanhood was captured for posterity in a small, plastic, sterilized cup.

I felt fearless on the day of the surgery. I knew the pain and my limp couldn't get any worse. It was pretty effortless to lie back, inhale the gas, and wait for everything to be corrected. And when I woke up, everything nearly was. The sensation was surreal. It's the same sensation you feel when you've been in a concert for hours and walk out into the quiet night.

Back then, patients were required to stay completely off their operated side for six weeks, so I spent the summer reading in my father's lumpy recliner. My parents hustled in and out for work, while I spent my days reading or watching movies they would start when they were in to check on me. Surgery is limiting, sure, but not as much as VHS tapes were.

They rented a freestanding potty chair, which was, essentially, a large plastic basin with legs. It stood beside my recliner. I would pull myself up by gripping the door frame, then pivot on my good leg, lower myself down, and shit in the bucket. Character building at its finest.

Even though the surgeon didn't typically recommend physical therapy after a hip replacement due to the age of most patients, my parents hired a therapist knowing that walking without a limp was paramount, as was dancing at prom. It would require a full summer of rigorous, physical work. Denise, a physical therapist and a longtime family friend, came to our house twice a week. Before we began our sessions, she would always spend time just chatting with me. I think on some level she understood that a girl going through puberty, while forced to sit in a recliner next to a bucket full of her own shit, just needed to talk.

Each week she'd give me a small, obtainable goal, like standing with a walker and lifting my operated leg out to the side for ten reps. When I had built up to that, she'd have me practice getting in and out of a chair without the cane. Later we worked on balance. And finally, one day, she told me I would be putting half my weight on my operated side.

My parents came home from work to watch. I stood in the dining room holding on to the walker, all my weight on my good side. I white-knuckled the walker as I slowly allowed my body to shift off the right side, and I finally put my foot down. I started my senior year of high school a few months later, and though I was finally pain-free, I was still just a bit wobbly on my new hip. But to me that was fine because everything on my insides—my character, my personality, my self-confidence—felt rock solid.

Years later, after receiving a promotion at the non-profit agency, I had to prioritize my new responsibilities. It was suggested I transfer Carey the Kangaroo to an intern or a high school volunteer. From there, Carey bounced around from interns to new hires and even to a few random employees who just wanted to see what it was like to bring the creature to life.

Every time I helped a newcomer into the suit, I demonstrated how to tuck in the mattress material so it wouldn't rub any skin and how to properly inflate the pouch. I'd explain how to turn on the nose fan, do the Carey wave to keep the gloves from falling off, and do the Godzilla walk to prevent tripping.

Most everyone was surprised at how heavy and hot the suit was and how little they could see. They were frustrated by how difficult it was to move about. And nearly every single inhabitant would want to know what to do if they started to get hot or dizzy or just tired of wearing the suit before an event was over.

The truth was, this was bound to happen. The body was heavy, limiting, and cumbersome. I could tell no one wanted to do this long-term. So when they asked for my advice on how to sustain the effort through an entire two-hour event out in the hot Oklahoma sun, I had knowledge to pull from. I'd remind them that there would be an icy cold beverage waiting at the end and encourage them to keep themselves cool—make smaller movements to retain energy, save smiling muscles for when the hood came off—basically, choose to focus on what's on the inside. And I'd always encourage them with the best part of all: when you feel you momentarily can't be yourself, choose to make the most of your character.

ALMOST EVERYTHING IS A CHOICE

Sure, some choices in life get made without our consent— to whom we are born, what we look like, tragedies that befall us. But it's important to remember that we are almost always given the biggest choice of all: how to react. The greatest choice we have before us is how to handle what happens to us. Sometimes it's how to react to those situations that are out of our control, and sometimes it's how we react to things we've had a hand in choosing.

I chose to go to graduate school in the same program I now administer. This is unique, for sure, but it also gives me great satisfaction to be part of helping others obtain a degree I took such pleasure in. When I took my position,

I couldn't wait to start recruiting students, knowing I was, for lack of a better term, selling them a great product.

Early on, I had a student who seemed overtly dissatisfied with the program. This not only baffled me, but it irritated me (I was new, mind you; I now handle apathetic students with aplomb). He never formally complained about the classes, any of the professors, or his classmates. But he seemed woefully apathetic—annoyed even—about his time in graduate school. This bothered me enough to mention it to my advisor. She laughed when I told her I had a student who didn't seem very invested. I went on to defend how great the program is and itemize all the great assignments, lectures, and experiences he was getting from our top-notch faculty members. "Meg," she laughed, "did you ever think that you loved the program so much because you *chose* to love it?"

I came to realize everyone was being given an equal experience, but not everyone was *receiving* an equal experience. Only those students who chose to enjoy their time, to be energized by their studies, and to be passionate about their program were fulfilled. Which is what I had been ten years earlier when I went through the program.

Psychologists Charles Carver and Michael Schreier study optimism. In their research, they find that optimism isn't just a trait we possess, but also a predictor of our behavior. They find that optimistic people tend to take more proactive steps to protect (or increase) their well-being and health. Beyond that, those who believe their efforts will result optimally are more likely to carry forth with the effort. If you think trying really hard in your job will result in a promotion, you're more likely to do good work. Which, you know, leads to a promotion.

Researcher John Gottman studied positivity in married couples. He found that the best predictor of a stable marriage came down to the ratio of positive and negative interactions between the spouses: The more positive interactions than negative, the more stable the marriage would predictably be. Later, researchers Marcial Losada and Emily Heaphy applied Gottman's conclusions to team dynamics in the workplace. They found similar outcomes. The power of a team—its effectiveness and productivity—didn't come down to skill set, education, or tenure in the job; it came down to the same ratio: The more positive interactions among team members, the better and stronger the team. This is great news for anyone who works in teams. Who cares if you don't know how to run the software needed? Just bring a winning smile!

But positivity doesn't just impact our well-being, actions, marriages, and coworkers; it also has a huge bearing on our health. A study conducted at Florida State University looked at whether a positive attitude had any effect on an athlete's ability to heal from sports-related injuries. Researchers looked specifically at a large group of college athletes with ankle and knee injuries. The researchers noticed that a small percentage of those studied (19 percent) recovered at a much faster rate. Accounting for similar health history and injury severity, those who recovered the quickest did three main things: goal-setting; positive self-talk; and healing imagery.

Studies like this point to the power of mental attitude. Not only can it shape our behaviors, strengthen our relationships, and improve our work, but it can help heal our bodies. I've had a broken leg before, so I know it took more than just a smile to heal from that, but there's ample evidence to support the concept that a good attitude can go a long way. And not just with the person standing next to you in the Starbucks line.

Vickie, a student of mine, came to see me one day about how unhappy she was at work. Beyond feeling frustrated by what she perceived was a dead-end job, Vickie was more bothered by the culture of her workplace.

"The morale is so low, I dread going to work every morning," she said. She explained that turnover in the top leadership and a few layoffs had led to so much uncertainty that the employees had all but given up. "We just kinda sit around and wait for the next bad thing to happen. They will probably take away our coffee machine next."

"So more than anything, you're upset the morale around the office is bad?" I asked.

"Yes!" she said. "I mean, this isn't my dream job, but even just being excited to go to work would help a lot."

"So, what are you doing to improve the morale?" I asked.

She looked at me quizzically for a beat before saying, "It's not my fault the morale is bad. And it's not my job to improve it."

"Then whose is it?" I asked.

A few months later I received an email from Vickie. In it she said that she realized her sour attitude was—even if in a small way—contributing to the low morale, and that it was her responsibility to do what she could to improve it. So she changed her mindset. She put her energy into her job, worked to energize those around her, and even stopped complaining to her friends and husband about her work. A few months after her mindset change, she landed an interview with an organization for which she'd long wanted to work, and was later offered the job.

I often find my students are waiting around for someone to change things for them—a boss, a friend, a spouse. But that change always starts with us and our reactions—and it always starts small. While Vickie didn't choose the turnover, layoffs, and bad morale at her company, she had the power to change at least part of it. Her case was a great example of how quickly people forget the choice—the power—they have over their situations. How we perceive and react to all that happens to us is one of the most powerful and substantial choices we make every day. Our attitude toward life—our friends, our work—creates an energy that is contagious. That change starts with us. And I've believed that since I was a kid.

• • •

I've always been naturally happy. That is one attribute I've never taken for granted. Just as people say that without your health you've got nothing, I feel the same about my happiness. Despite my own struggles with overthinking it—or what some might call high-functioning, mild anxiety—I've long been secure in the happiness I feel from within. And among all things I must protect, my own happiness is at the top of the list, mostly because I'm the only one able to fight for it. And I've known that since one particular, somewhat mundane moment in the middle of a lazy summer. It is a moment upon which my entire life has been based.

I was only ten years old, riding my bike slowly up and down our mile-long driveway in a worn camp T-shirt and gym shorts. Given my physical limitations at the time, I had perfected the one-legged pedal in which I would pump hard with my right leg while my left leg dangled out to the side, my foot mere inches above the ground.

I was waiting on my friend Kate to arrive for a sleepover, and her mom's van would be pulling around the corner at any minute. As I swerved slowly back and forth along the gravel, I thought about our plans for that day. Kate and I had decided we would spend the entire afternoon down by the large creek that ran behind my house. And, as we always did, we would stay up late that night, talk, and perhaps prank call a few friends. My foot peddled faster the more I thought about how much fun we were going to have. My best friend, a hot summer day full of exploring in the fresh country air, and the thrill of staying up late. I stopped my bike a few yards from the end of the driveway. I was trying to process my excitement. Even at that young age I realized what I was feeling was something phenomenal. It was pure happiness, and I wanted it to last as long as possible.

I put out the kickstand of my bike, got off, and paced a while on the driveway. How could I keep this feeling? Kate was only staying one night, I realized. What could I do tomorrow to feel this full of hope, energy, and joy? I thought long and hard, searching my brain quickly as I wanted to get this figured out before I saw Kate's van pull around the corner. Oh! I remembered, the following evening my dad was going to take us to the local baseball game, and my mom had agreed to pack a picnic. My mind kept going. What about the next day? What could keep this level up so that after Kate left, and after the baseball game, I'd always have something for the following day?

Before I could figure out what might follow the baseball game, I saw the van. I yelled out in excitement, jumped back on my bike, kicked up the stand, and peddled hard beside the vehicle, Kate laughing and waving from the back seat, as it made its way down the winding driveway toward my house. As I worked hard to keep up, I promised myself this: I would always find something to look forward to.

This became the practice of my youth: looking around for something to anticipate. The start of school, a slumber party, a movie, a birthday present, my sister coming home from college. I'd spend a few minutes each day consciously cataloguing what I was excited about. After a while, I didn't have to stop and do it; I just became a person always looking forward to something. If there wasn't something to anticipate, I'd create something. A new project, time with friends, a good book. This became so fluid that much of my marriage now centers on this concept: create carrots in our relationship. A date, a trip, streaming a good show, trying a new restaurant. My husband and I put incentives in our path to get us through tough, hectic workweeks—perhaps a bottle of wine on Friday to celebrate. Or something to anticipate so we can get through a busy month—maybe a babysitter and a night out.

This concept was the key to our success on a recent family vacation. Determined to have a good trip, I realized that the concept I discovered at the age of ten was the perfect way to make it happen. Jim and I went to The Dollar Store and purchased ten dollars' worth of trinkets: Slinkys, rubber balls, ponies with hair you could brush, coloring books, and a variety of other silly little prizes. On the eve of the trip, we told our girls they would get a prize for every block of time they were good—every hour during the car ride, each bathroom stop where they washed their hands, and stretches of time in which they didn't subject us to one of their epic fits. This was an intriguing proposal to our negotiation-prone children.

On the road, an hour into our trip, I handed each girl a little toy car. They squealed in delight and played happily in their car seats for the next hour, after which they were each given a tiny, plastic snake. These prizes became the pattern of the trip. In the beginning, my oldest was desperate to know what the next prize was, almost unable to control her excitement. But after a few, she became more patient with each trinket. On our way home after three days, and having earned handfuls of new, tiny treats,

Lowery made a comment as we turned the corner onto our street. "I really liked waiting for my prizes. I was the most excited right before you gave one to me."

Before my students graduate, they always bemoan the fact that they will miss school. They claim it's because they love learning—and that's certainly part of it; people love who they are when they are learning. But a bigger part of it is the structured anticipation, which is the defining characteristic of school. Students look forward to the first day of class. They are eager to see who else will be there and what the teacher will be like. Soon, they find themselves immersed in schoolwork, busy with readings and assignments. They look forward to getting through the midterm, and they anticipate spring break. They await the return to the classroom. Then they find themselves gearing up for finals week, and they can't wait to celebrate the beginning of semester break. This process repeats itself over and over. School is the template for having something to look forward to. Of course, students cringe when school ends—in part because they will miss the learning, but also because they will miss the anticipation of what is just around the corner.

When I entered the working world, I was saddened by how little there was to anticipate. There were the bank holidays, of course, but nothing like the structured anticipation to which I had grown accustomed during the first twenty-two years of my life. I sometimes wonder whether I went back to graduate school as much for the field of study as I did for the regimented expectations. I'm sure it was both, but it's also no surprise that I still haven't left.

At the end of that summer when I was ten years old, our daily newspaper was looking for kids to interview for a back-to-school feature. Every day for a week leading up to school, kids were asked about the fun they had over the summer. While playing at my friend Cassie's house, the editor of the paper stopped by to get our picture and a few quotes (doesn't get more small-town than that). She took a picture of Cassie and then one of me, sitting on the porch swing. Then she took out a pad of paper and asked Cassie to pick the most fun thing she had done that summer. Cassie responded, "Our family's trip to Disney World!" The editor then turned to me and asked the same question, to which I responded, "I had fun every day."

A few days later, when school started up, I overheard Cassie making fun of me for what I had said in the paper. I brushed this off because, well, Cassie hadn't actually gone to Disney World that summer, or ever—she just made it up, I guess to impress the tens of readers of our sleepy town's newspaper. And, also, I *did* have fun every day. I *made* fun every day. As a ten-year-old, I made the most important discovery of my life: Happiness was a choice I could make. This was not only the key to enjoying my childhood, but it was a great foundation for overcoming many things that were ahead of me in life: heartbreak, financial stress, postpartum depression, the *Friends* finale. I just have to find things that excite me, energize me, and fill me with joy. They are all around me. I just have to keep turning the corner.

THIS RELATIONSHIP IS A CHOICE

Of all the choices we are afforded, the one people continually underestimate is their relationships. Who we choose to spend our time with is a fundamental choice upon which all our other choices (and wants) in life rest. How much time and energy have you given to bad relationships? Not just romantic ones, but friendships. And for how many reasons do you feel obligated to maintain relationships? You grew up together, you share a history, he helped you through a bad breakup, she saved you from a burning house (actually, she might be a keeper), you were roommates in college, you both love *Game of Thrones*. There are so many reasons to keep people in our lives without asking the question to which we always know the answer: Am I happy?

Now maybe that sounds too simple. But most every choice in life *is* that simple. Do you feel good after time spent with this person? Yes or no? It doesn't mean that every single time you see them it's always laughter and sunshine. Sometimes she's saving you from a burning building for shit's sake! But overall, you should have people in your life whom you are always eager to see. I cannot say that's been true of every relationship in my life. And it's most certainly not always true for the students who seek out my advice on their friendships and relationships.

• • •

Kristin stayed seated long after everyone else left the class. I gathered my books and notes at the lectern, and then I asked whether she needed anything before I left. When she looked up, I could tell she was crying. I put my bag and books down and walked to the back of the room to sit beside her. I didn't know her well. We had never spoken outside of the classroom. I knew only what she had shared in class, which was a little about her career and that she was newly married. "How can I help?" I asked. She swallowed hard before she spoke. "I don't think my marriage is going well."

When I probed her to tell me more, she explained how she never thought her relationship seemed quite right; she was nervous to get married—just three months earlier— but her parents and friends had assured her everything would get better after the wedding. (I can't tell you how many times I've heard something like this.) She told me all the issues that existed between them as a couple and with them as individuals. Then she asked me whether marriage should be so hard, so incredibly complicated.

I'm no relationship expert. A guy I sometimes hung out with told me, over the phone, we could no longer be together because I didn't share his same religious beliefs. I paused for a moment before responding with, "I'm sorry, I wasn't even aware we were dating." Aside from vague relationships, I've also been entangled in some unhealthy relationships, some exciting but pointless relationships, and some painfully mediocre relationships. But, I *can* say that now, my marriage is a highlight of my life. Not because of luck or fate—nothing nearly that complicated or mystical. I think the most complex constructs in life, like love and relationships, are made up of simple truths. Even in the most intricate Lego castle, the individual pieces are nothing more than basic building blocks. But we tend to make relationships messy. We build them up to be intricate and complicated and then fail to recognize the simple components. There are three building blocks I look for when identifying and maintaining healthy relationships, be they friendship, familial, or romantic. And, on the instances in which a student of mine has sought me out for relationship advice, here's what I say:

1. The Best Has Already Come

I dated a guy in high school who was extremely into hunting. His passion for shooting animals was not unusual among the people with whom I grew up in rural Oklahoma. It's important to note that I had a moral issue with hunting, and yet, we began dating in the fall. We went on one solid date before the opening of deer season. He was willing to make time for me during the week, but on the weekends he was busy with his bow. At the close of deer season, I started to get excited because I knew that would mean we would see each other more and that the strain I was feeling in this new relationship would go away.

I was talking this over with a friend one day, explaining how relieved I was that my relationship could finally get some momentum. She shot me a doubtful look and said, "In my experience, whatever the relationship is like *right now* is the best it is ever going to be." I brushed this off, of course, as I was seventeen and believed I was just one buck shot to a deer's ass away from being whisked off my feet. And yet, I learned, a week later, turkey season was starting. That relationship didn't make it to Thanksgiving. I later dated a few guys in college where I had that same "just after [life distraction] it will be better" feeling. Just after finals week. Just after March Madness. Just after, just after, just after.

Eventually, I came to realize the advice my friend had given me was quite profound, and it has been incredibly useful in sizing up the potential of a relationship. There are always, and will always be, distractions and crises in life. Those may not be the most *enjoyable* times in a relationship, but even in the misery or uncertainty of the situation, you should be able to clearly see how the relationship stands up against adversity.

The weeks after the birth of our firstborn were among the toughest I've ever endured. Postpartum depression had sunk me like a rock into water. I was depressed and afraid in a way I couldn't quite articulate to my husband, and he was concerned for me in a way he hadn't yet experienced. But we remained strong and united. Even in the face of a very challenging time, I never thought, *Just after I get past this terrible feeling, our* relationship *will be better*. Now, our stress level, our ability to raise our child, and our sleeping patterns all stood to improve. But our relationship, even during that tough time, was still a source of comfort and love.

Rare is the case that a relationship starts extremely rocky, with jealous bouts, loads of fighting, or a lack of trust, only to later blossom into something healthy and wonderful. I mean, I'm sure it *does* happen. But waiting that out is almost never worth the gamble. (And further, there's no need to compromise your principles. If, for example, you are opposed to hunting, perhaps don't date a hunter.) A few of my students have been in relationships in which they didn't exactly know what the other person was thinking, where they stood, or where the relationship was going. That isn't a good sign, because if the other person can't make you feel secure in the relationship now, they aren't going to be much better at it in a few months, a few years, or after you say, "I do." Look at a relationship as it *currently* is; that's the single best predictor of where it is going.

2. Better or Worse

I had a friend who was quite the bully. I didn't realize it, but every time I was with her I felt on the defense—for what, I'm still not sure. After a dinner or a round of drinks with her, I would come home beaten down. Jim pressed me on why I continued to accept her behavior or why I felt the friendship was worth continuing to invest in. As always, I stressed the history between us, the breakup she had helped me through years ago, and the many memories we had together. Jim would always shrug and say, "But a friend should never make you feel worse."

Often, in friendships and relationships, seeing this is difficult. Or, perhaps it is just forgotten. But Jim was right. Friends, family, lovers, spouses...whatever the relationship, they should be the very people who make you feel the best about yourself. I mean, they should also challenge you, but they shouldn't be against you. For the most part, being around people who lift you up is perhaps the most basic goal of all. A simple little building block. After all, we get to choose with whom we spend our time and our energy. We must choose wisely.

I was nervous the first time I had to teach a college course. I remember being concerned that the students would be against me. Maybe I would come into the classroom on the first day as the enemy (this was not the case; I wouldn't be their enemy until midterms). But as I walked to class, I was struck with a comforting thought: After it was over, I would get to go home to Jim. And no matter what happened in class (chalk being thrown at my face or, perhaps, laughter at my choice of blazer), he would be happy to see me. No matter how poorly I did in front of the class, Jim would take the stance that I was great, and everyone else was ridiculous to respond with chalk throwing and blazer-shaming. In that moment I realized how simple it was to choose the people I'd have in my corner: those who are on my side. Students be damned! I had a cheerleader at home.

Having a spouse, friends, or family who are on your side is the best defense against all that can hit you in everyday life. But it's easy to forget this and hold onto relationships and friendships that make us feel worse—that make us feel bad about ourselves or, worst of all, make us think we need to improve before we can receive the love that deep down we already know we deserve.

Does your partner/friend/sister/waiter make you feel better or worse about yourself? After time together, do you leave with a smile on your face, or a frown? It couldn't be any simpler. Don't make it hard on yourself. And don't let anyone else make it hard on you, either.

3. Keeping the Stakes Low

In college, I briefly dated a guy whom I felt needed me to act a certain way. Not too chatty, not too bubbly. If I became either, he'd call me on it. One day he picked me up and seemed mad. "Are you okay?" I asked, touching him lightly on the arm. He sighed heavily. "You ask me that *all* the time. I wish you'd stop it." I sat awkwardly beside him in the car trying to figure out how many times during our few weeks of dating I had asked if he was okay. I tried to comprehend why asking that was so upsetting. Was it *how* I said it? Or just that I asked at all? For the next few weeks, I tried really hard not to ask again. I spent so much time worried if he was okay and wondering *when* it was okay to ask if he was okay, and in what *way* to ask if he was okay, that I completely forgot to ask myself if I was okay. When I finally did, it was clear I wasn't, and I ended the relationship. This kind of tension can arise in other relationships—not just romantic ones—where every action is high stakes. Those people who always seem to be testing you and, perhaps, waiting for you to fail.

I carried a little of that desperation into my marriage. One night, I unexpectedly had to work late at an event and my cell phone had died. I felt guilty for being out at an event, even a work event, without having the chance to let Jim know I'd be late. When I finally came rushing through the front door, I was worried Jim would be mad

I was later than I had promised and without knowing where I'd been. He was happy to see me. I confessed my concern. "Hey, the stakes aren't that high," he said. "The best thing about us is the stakes are always low." It was the first time I'd ever heard him say that, but it so clearly defined what I loved most about our relationship. There was no test. There was no monitoring. It was perhaps the first relationship in which I experienced what low stakes felt like. It was a refreshingly freeing feeling. Our love and our life together are absolutely high stakes, of course. But the stakes *between us* are super low. The assumption is good intentions from either side. The default is trust. It would take a great deal to unravel that because each moment between us is low pressure. There's a breathe-easy quality about that kind of relationship.

Kristin divorced her husband a few months after that night we talked in the classroom. Then she moved to the West Coast, developed a valuable product for the mortgage industry, and started a company that is now wildly successful. Every time I hear from her she's traveling in a different part of the globe. About a year after she graduated, she reached out to say she was coming back into town and asked whether I would have time to meet her.

When she walked into my office, she looked completely different. Some of that was her California tan, but a lot, she said, was being free of her bad marriage. "When I talked to you about my marriage that night," she said, "I was convinced the problems in my relationship were so incredibly complicated that they couldn't be solved." I nodded, remembering how much she had struggled to explain her pain and sadness to me. "But," she sighed with a smile, "it turns out relationships are only ever as complicated as we build them up to be."

Relationships *can* be tricky, messy, and complicated, but they don't *need* to be. We are in control of our lives, which means we are in control of whom we let into our lives. This isn't to say there won't be hard times, tough disagreements, or unforeseen circumstances. But in general, the most complicated of relationships and friendships can be understood if we allow ourselves to see their basic building blocks and perhaps the most basic component of all: In this relationship are you happy, or are you not? It really is that simple.

THERE IS NO *ONE* CHOICE

Most people are seeking a destination, and very rarely is it geographical. People convince themselves that "if *this*, then *that*." If they can get more money, then they can finally feel less stressed. If they can get their degree, then they can get their dream job. If they could just poop alone, then they would have no complaints about motherhood.

It doesn't work like that, though. When people finally reach that destination, they find themselves looking toward another one. I once got to poop alone and then I thought, "If my kids would change out the toilet paper rolls, then I could more fully enjoy this." When we get what we want, we tend to keep wanting.

This is called the Diderot effect. Denis Diderot was an eighteenth century French writer who received a beautiful scarlet dressing gown as a gift. Because he was quite broke, this gown was the nicest thing he owned. He had longed his whole life for something so beautiful. Rather than being grateful and excited for the new possession, he realized he needed additional things to accommodate his gown. For instance, he couldn't wipe his quill on this beautiful gown as he had his old tattered clothes, so he would need to buy some handkerchiefs. He could no longer sit in the same splintered chair; it might rip the new gown. And on and on it went; acquiring one nice thing makes you want for more. Like that time my husband bought me a nice pair of shiny, red rain boots for my birthday. I simply couldn't wear them without a new stylish trench coat.

Everyone struggles with the Diderot effect to some extent. This isn't always bad, of course—achieving something in life leads to more achievements; once you earn the degree, you want a better job. But more than achieving or acquiring, people are striving to feel content in life, work, love, and parenthood. It's easy to think the path to contentment *is* achieving and acquiring. I've had more students than I can count say, "If I can just graduate this program with a 4.0, I'll finally feel proud of myself." We do this all the time in small and big ways. We pin *everything* on *one* thing. And never once has one thing been everything.

• • •

I spend an inordinate amount of time on Zillow looking at beach houses. This is because I deeply fantasize about one day achieving a level of success, and—more important—satisfaction with that success, that I'll be able to spend the rest of my life living near water and relaxing for much of the day.

This fantasy is so intense, I finally had to confess it to Jim; I was afraid he'd look at my Internet search history and see that Googling "affordable Cape Cod mansions" is all I ever really do on my computer. He thought this was a nice idea, and a dream he would certainly share in, but it was obvious to him that it was so unobtainable there was no point in having an entire laptop devoted to the cause.

Jim gave me a dose of reality by explaining that the $6.4 million harbor home I had my eyes on was perhaps just a bit outside our price range. So I chose to reframe my goal. I decided that the large lake an hour from where we currently live must certainly have homes for sale that are more affordable.

Indeed, I found some. I made Jim and the girls crowd around my laptop to flip through pictures of lake cottages overlooking an expansive aquatic horizon. Still not believing that Jim was as invested in this dream as I was, I made a call to a real estate agent and set up a series of house showings. While in the second house of the day, our oldest looked up at me and said, "What are we even doing here?" To which Jim responded, "This is your mother's goal: to work so hard, she can finally relax."

I've noticed that most of my issues as a highly ambitious and intensely motivated individual were based on the idea that there was, in fact, a golden ticket, a single achievement, status, or tasteful twelve-room beach house, in which I would finally feel satisfied.

On the day of my dissertation defense—which is a highly emotional and surreal experience for anyone—I emerged from the room, kissed my husband, and declared, "I'm done. Not just with school, but with having to go after something big. I've proved everything and anything I've ever needed to prove to myself, and I can finally relax."

My husband hugged me proudly, with tears in his eyes, and said, "Oh, Meg. That's great of you to say. But I'm going to put a clock on that. Let's see how long you can go." Two weeks later I announced I would be writing a book.

Many of the meetings I have with students, current or prospective, pivot around the idea that a golden ticket exists. Current students are sometimes convinced that if they don't take the policy course that is offered in the spring, then they won't be able to go after the job they have their eye on. As if hiring managers dig deep down into transcripts and review course syllabi.

Prospective students always ask what they can do with the degree once they earn it. I often reply, "Not a damn thing. Or, everything. Your call." The degree, sadly, is not a golden ticket. I cannot guarantee anyone anything. I can assure them they will have a good experience and that they will learn a lot, but their diploma will not be an express ticket on a train to success.

Even my children live in a world where the streets are paved with golden tickets. My oldest believes that if she can just have one piece of leftover Halloween candy after dinner, she will be happy. My youngest follows a similar line of thought—perhaps genetic, but probably environmental—that if we give her just one blanket, she will lie down and go to sleep. But then later she's convinced it's a stuffed animal that she needs. And yet, the stuffed animal also needs a blanket. And what about a glass of water? One more song?

Each girl is living in a world they construct, and convince us of, where there's one thing that will solve the problem. Tame the beast. But, as is almost always the case, that beast is within us.

We all find ourselves searching for the thing that's going to fix it all. I've lost count of how often I say things at home like, "If I can just get the house clean enough, I can relax." Or, "If I just do better at meal planning, cooking each night won't be as stressful." Or, as I'm known to say frequently, "If I just get to a point in my career and life where I'm satisfied, I can buy a mansion on the beach and relax."

See, the problem with my beach house idea, a problem Jim has always recognized but is too kind to point out, is that a person like me will never be satisfied in life and work. There is no end point, satisfaction point, or any one thing that will ultimately be good enough, lasting enough, or satisfying enough. In fact, the only person who would be able to reach that point in their career is an apathetic and lazy person. How is an apathetic and lazy person ever going to work hard enough to buy a beach house?

And so it goes.

I remind my students that there's no single class that will make or break the entire degree program. And there's no degree program that will make or break an entire career. All anything ever is and ever will be is an investment in ourselves, a declaration of what we care about, what interests us, and how we choose to devote our time.

My daughters are never going to eat enough candy to feel satisfied. Sick to their stomachs, maybe, but no single Fun Size Snickers is ever going to make Lowery go to bed without a fight. And no single blanket, book, or bunny is going to make London feel comforted enough to just lie the hell down and go to sleep.

And a beach house on Cape Cod would never truly satisfy me. I mean, I have a really good idea for how I would decorate the lookout perch and what I would do with the seventh bedroom, but then I know I'd run around saying, "If I can just get all 12,000 square feet of it clean, I can go relax at the beach today." And when I look back at all the decisions I've made, goals I've achieved, and people I've had in my life, it will be clear to see there was no single thing that defines it all. Instead, it will be an entire life experience that's just the ticket.

UNDERSTAND YOUR CHOICE CYCLE

After years of listening to students wrestle with life choices, I became aware of a common, self-induced choice cycle. Kaitlyn was in my office one day, agonizing over a choice: staying in her current job—which she loved—or taking a new position that had more potential for growth. She was so afraid that she'd make the wrong decision.

She had earned a degree to get her the job she currently had. She had worked hard at it and felt she was not only effective, but respected. But, as people tend to do, she was itchy for options. She agonized over whether to even apply for a job she found that had piqued her interest. It took a while to convince her that applying and accepting are two different choices. So she applied. Then, after the interview, she spent days mulling over whether the job was a good fit. Eventually, she decided she was happy where she was and turned down the second job when it was offered to her.

Her self-induced choice cycle is as common as they come. People start to feel as if they don't have enough choices (and without ample choice, how can they get all they want out of life?). They long for more options, but often agonize about seeking them out. Then they struggle when choices are presented to them. People experience a lack of choice as stifling, and an abundance of choice as overwhelming.

The body of research on decision-making and decision theory is deep and interesting. Much of it centers around how humans make choices, what motivates those choices, and what factors influence those choices. Most of this kind of research is based in the field of economics because the market wants to know what you'll buy, when you'll buy it, and why you'll buy it. For example, you may currently *want* some food, but what will you choose to eat? I'm sure General Mills wants to know how I make a decision among the company's variety of delicious breakfast cereals. Trust me, it's a toughie. But beyond that, decision theory seeks to explain the rationality, probability, utility, reasoning, predictability, behavior, moral judgment, and even group influence of human choice. That's the thing about our choices—they are difficult to analyze and predict because, well, humans are tricky.

Humans are tricky because we aren't exactly rational, at least according to psychologists Daniel Kahneman and Amos Tversky, who discovered cognitive biases, which is a term to describe how humans systematically make choices that deviate from clear logic. Of course we do! We humans are influenced by a variety of factors, not least of which are our upbringing, social circle, and emotions. We are influenced by the idea that we should constantly be doing and wanting more. Just think about something you were desperate for in your past that you now have in your present. It feels good to have it, sure. Yet I'd wager you have more wants in your future. It's difficult to understand why suddenly we feel itchy for more choices. When we get what we want we almost always want for more. Sometimes we can't explain why we need to do something—change a major, quit a job, move cities, wear a beret. But because we aren't truly logical creatures—at least not when it comes to the choices we make—it's difficult to understand when and why we get into the choice cycle. Whereby we seek out choices, run screaming when we get choices, and are remorseful when choices diminish.

One thing that helps the cycle of choice is to understand what choices are and what they aren't. Choices *are* overwhelming. But they *aren't* precious. Some choices carry more weight—the person to marry, or a pixie cut, for example. But overall, choices aren't precious. Rest assured, you get lots and lots of them. In fact, some of those choices are chances to alter previous choices if you chose wrong—divorces, or hair extensions, for example. But your number of choices are not finite, and most choices certainly aren't final.

Further, choices *aren't* punishments, but rewards. If you are in a place in which you get to bring choices into your life, you're essentially earning a reward. Further, if you bring yourself options that are difficult to choose among, you've hit the jackpot. If your life is such that you can seek out options that are essentially equal (you aren't choosing between a new car and *death*, for example), then you are doing something right. After all, choices are a thing of privilege. Some of that privilege you were given, but most of it you have earned. Acknowledge and respect it.

Kaitlyn was making a choice between two great options: a job she had and was good at, or a job with new challenges. Getting to make that choice was a reward for her hard work and current stability. As she agonized over it, I had to remind her that, while this decision *was* important, she was choosing between two *great* options— a realistic and positive game of Would You Rather. Not only that, but she would have lots of other options. She was already forgetting she was having to choose between two jobs because *she* had applied.

See choices for what they are: endless rewards for moving through your life. Don't ever fear or avoid them. Understand exactly why you are in the choice cycle, but never wish for the cycle to stop. The interesting aspect of choice is that, regardless of what choices we are weighing, there are some universal truths in how we approach each one.

• • •

During my freshman year of college, I was astounded by the seemingly endless opportunities available for students: the clubs, parties, jobs, friends. There were so many decisions to make. So rather than actually make any, I just accepted everything college had to offer. I not only carried more than a full load of classes working toward three majors, but I signed up to be a member of numerous clubs, officers in some, and there was one I even started myself. I worked two on-campus jobs and had my eyes set on studying abroad my junior year. Then, as I can't adequately express the influence the show *Felicity* had on me, I decided to apply to be a resident advisor (RA) in the dorms.

I was surprised and energized by the rigorous interview process to become an RA. I sat in a room with all the current RAs, the hall directors, and the director of housing. I was questioned for hours and gave solutions to the hypothetical scenarios they provided. I ran through sets of tires and did pushups in the rain. Then the other RAs sat around me in a circle and told me what my life would really be like as an RA: the hours, the weekends, student suicide attempts and eating disorders, kicking boys out after curfew, and cleaning up some disgusting messes. Exactly what Noel so beautifully portrayed in season one.

I was offered a position two days later. Though I had worked hard to prepare for the interview, and I knew what a true honor it was to be offered the position, I was still unsure whether I would accept the offer. In a rare move, I called my brother for advice. I told him about the interview process, the exclusivity of the offer, and how great it would look on a resume. When I was finished, he said only this: "Just leave time to actually enjoy college." After we hung up, I immediately called the hall director and turned down the job. I'm so glad I did because I enjoyed the hell out of college.

Of the various reasons college students want to meet with me now as an academic advisor, there is one in particular that recurs regularly: contemplating a PhD. In any given month I meet with at least five people who are interested in earning a doctorate. Often these are students of mine, but, increasingly, I get meeting requests from community members who want to ask about the process. I try to take all these meetings because I want to give people some perspective no one gave me when I was weighing the possibility of a PhD.

I'm usually the kind to suggest everyone can have anything and everything they want out of this life—and I do believe that. But the PhD is a tricky goal to champion. It's one of those choices that people can only entertain at a certain point of privilege, which means that nearly every person contemplating one is capable and has the means to go after it. So I spend my time in these advising sessions talking people through why they have put this particular choice on their table. Generally, there are four archetypes among those contemplating a doctorate. I've found that with most every major decision (be it a PhD, a different job, or a new house), people seem to justify decisions in similar patterns.

1. Filling the Void

I met a girl named Sara one afternoon for lunch after a mutual friend suggested we meet. I could immediately size up that Sara was kind, funny, and sharp. She was on the verge of completing her undergraduate degree and was considering going for a doctorate. In these scenarios— where I'm meeting the person for the first time—I like to listen for the excitement in their voice. Often, people have this voice when they mention their family or a project they are working on. But for Sara, I couldn't hear it while she talked about getting a PhD. So I tried to take our conversation down different paths until I did. Eventually, while talking about her volunteer work with intercity kids, I heard her voice rise slightly, so I called her on it. I told her she sounded way more excited about her volunteer work than about getting a PhD. She laughed and admitted that she really didn't want to pursue a PhD, but she knew she *needed* to. I corrected her: No one *needs* to do anything, let alone get a PhD. Then she sat up straight and got a serious look on her face. "Well," she said, "if I had it, I would get the respect I know I deserve in meetings."

And there it was. A PhD would solve her feelings of inadequacy during meetings at her corporate job. Or, more generally, a PhD would fill a void she felt that was deep within, and a sense of insecurity. She was willing to go down a path she wasn't even excited about for the false promise of respect, something she felt she could never achieve on her own. I smiled and said, "Sara, if a PhD got you automatic respect, I'd be able to tell you that no one has been disrespectful to me since I graduated. But as I think you can guess, that simply isn't true."

Sara is not the only person who believed that the doctorate degree would earn her a level of respect and admiration, make her feel better about her status or her intellect, alleviate an insecurity, or fill an internal void (from what you feel or what others say). Of those I talk to about a PhD, it's typically women who have this motivation. Women have to fight harder for respect and admiration. The scrutiny placed on women is far greater than the scrutiny of their male counterparts. A woman in politics, for example, has to be smart, relatable, *and* attractive. She must look maternal *and* tough; youthful *and* wise. Men can generally get away with just one of those qualities. Women must try harder, do more, and be better than their male peers to even have a seat at the table. So it's no wonder that women seek out training and education at much higher rates than men. And while education and skill-building can make a woman stronger and smarter, it's also not always required to keep going after more and more credentials. A PhD is a big goal, and a big thing to accomplish, but it's not big enough to fill a void.

2. Climbing Mount Everest

Jason was a good student of mine. He was curious, engaged, always excited to debate politics in class, and eager to have me challenge his opinions. He was a strong writer and a critical thinker, so it didn't surprise me when he requested a meeting to talk about going on for a PhD. As I always do with meetings like this, I warned him that I was going to push back hard on his desire for one, and if, in the end, he was still up for the degree, he'd have my unconditional support.

We talked for nearly an hour about the details of a PhD that are fuzzy for most before they apply. Unlike his master's, he'd need to be a full-time student—as in *not* have an income. He'd get a small university stipend, if he could secure one, and would devote anywhere from four to seven years to his studies. This meant four to seven years without contributing to a 401k (I wish someone had told me that one). Then we talked about how the job market works and how he would be at the mercy of the positions available, potentially moving across the country to take a job. The more I talked about these challenges, the more excited Jason became. He was practically salivating when I showed him the dismal job outlook statistics for a recent PhD graduate. Finally, after his eyes were wider than my kids' on Christmas morning, I said, "Jason, you seem really excited by the challenges." He nodded feverishly and explained how much fun the challenges sounded. "And," he exclaimed, "I'll be so damn proud when I am done!"

I laughed, amused at his tenacity. But then I sat there quietly for a minute. "Jack," I spoke carefully, "a PhD isn't your Mount Everest, is it?" His smile faded instantly. He was quiet for a few beats. "Yes," he finally admitted. "Is that not okay?"

Sure, it's okay to want to set massive goals and try to obtain them. But there was no part of me (or of Jason) that thought he wasn't going to be successful. He was already an exemplary student, so he was already mastering graduate school. How much of a challenge would a PhD be? Further, the thrill of climbing Everest ends. And I'm sure a vast majority of people who get to the top and live to tell about it find themselves searching for the next big challenge a short while later. A PhD is not a mountain to climb. It's not a stake in the ground that represents anything about you. A PhD is not a metric of strength, smarts, or ambition. If anything, it's simply a measure of mental stamina— something you can test in a multitude of other ways every day. Not only that, but a PhD costs money and time, and it takes you down a specific career path. It sticks to you a bit more than heroically climbing up the mountain.

After a few months, Jason came to meet with me again. He was calmer and a bit more clearheaded. He said it was obvious that he was looking at the PhD as a chance to prove something to himself and, if he thought about it, that wasn't enough of a reason to uproot his family or give up his nice income. Ultimately, Jason decided the PhD really was just his Mount Everest. So he scrapped the plan. Last I heard from him, he's still gainfully employed and currently enrolled in mountain climbing classes.

3. Having a Safety Net

Rainy was in a different graduate program than the one I administer, but she had taken a few of my classes. She asked to meet with me one day to talk about what she should do after graduation. I knew this was probably a PhD meeting.

I was right, but she wasn't seeking my advice on whether to get one. She wanted to ask for my opinions on certain programs and to see if I'd write a letter of recommendation for her. She was bright and younger than most people in graduate school. In fact, unlike most of her peers, she'd come directly into her master's program after earning her bachelor's. This meant she had never had a job. Not ever. She'd always been a student.

I listened as she talked about which programs she was looking into and what she needed me to address in her letter. After she stopped talking, I put my hands up. "Rainy, I just want to ask you one question: Are you doing a PhD because you are scared to no longer be a student?" She paused for a moment, burst into tears, and said, "I'm terrified!" She explained that all her peers in graduate school were in the middle of their careers. She saw that everyone had skills, important titles, and lots of responsibility. It both impressed and intimidated her. "But Rainy," I said, "They are also about fifteen years older than you. You can't have what they have unless you try."

Rainy wasn't alone in her fear. Students, if they are good, tend to wrap their identities up in their studies. They know they are good at school, so they want that to keep going. They are, on one hand, comfortable in their ability to excel in academics; and on the other hand, convinced they couldn't be good at anything else. The problem with that is school does eventually end. Unless the plan is to finish the PhD; go to medical school, law school, and seminary; and retire in dental school, avoiding the working world isn't a good idea because it isn't possible. And, you know, you still gotta pay those student loans somehow.

In my experience, students who excel in school don't excel because somehow they are only good at school. They excel because they are motivated and engaged individuals. So, when they go out into the working world with the same motivation and engagement, they are equally successful. Whether it's school or some other comfort zone, don't stay in it just because you're good at it. Because all you'll really end up learning is that it has to end sometime.

4. Seeking Permission

Tanner crossed paths with my husband in a professional capacity. During their time working together, she told Jim she was contemplating a PhD, so Jim suggested she reach out to me. I knew of her only through my husband, but I was happy to meet with her one day in my office. She was assertive, kind, and funny. She had finished her master's program a few years earlier and was fairly sure she was ready for a doctorate. One point in her favor was that her company was willing to pay for it. That's a big load off right there.

We talked through her professional and educational background and then I asked her what she wanted to do in the next phase of her career. She explained that she wanted to work in public policy, specifically in education. I said, "And why do you need the PhD to do that?" She smiled and said, "Well, until I have that degree, I won't be taken seriously in the field."

A number of my students who want to go on for a PhD are students who "want to work in policy." And to them I always say, "So go work in policy." They always look at me, confused, and say, "But I can't without a PhD." Many are convinced they need a stamp on their resume that allows them to do the kind of work they want to do. When I pressed Tanner on her belief that she needed a PhD to do her job, she shrugged and said, "I just assumed you did. I mean, don't you?" And I told her what I tell anyone who has this misconception: nope.

Now, if she wanted to be an academic who *researched* policy, you bet she'd need a PhD. And that's really all a PhD is—a chance to be in academia as a researcher or a faculty member. But if a student wants to *influence* policy, *create* policy, or help *implement* better policy, a PhD is not required. If a student came to me and said, "I want to go to welding school because I want to be a welder," I would say, "That's a great reason. Go for it." But the belief people carry that a PhD is the permission they need to do something, govern something, produce something, or *mean* something is false. When advising students like Tanner, who believe they need a PhD to do what they need to do or are already doing, I remind them that it is always better to beg for forgiveness than to assume you need permission.

Decisions we make are often predicated on the pressures we feel, whether we are trying to obtain a certain status we hold dear, trying to prove something to ourselves or others, trying to avoid change, or convinced we can't do what we want to do without permission. Decisions are always made through the lens of our own insecurities, bias, and perception of how we think we are perceived.

Contemplating a PhD is a decision I frequently talk through with students, but the same pattern of thought can happen regardless of what decision is being weighed. Sometimes we are seeking something in our life (maybe a significant other, maybe a cat) to fill a void. Often we are trying to prove something to ourselves (maybe wanting to break up with someone to show you're capable of being alone). Sometimes we are trying not to rock the boat (maybe staying in a job you hate for stability). And sometimes we are seeking the approval of others (maybe your parents, maybe your butcher). The point is, we can bring a lot of emotion and pressure into our decisions. I don't regret my PhD or wish I had gone down a different path. I find where I am professionally to be fulfilling and exciting. But that doesn't mean that if I *hadn't* gotten a PhD, I wouldn't be saying the same about wherever my career path took me.

I take comfort in a night out I once had nearly ten years after graduating college. Two of my college friends came to visit. Both were RAs in college, and one was my RA during my freshman year. Though we hadn't seen each other since college, we immediately fell back into our old rhythm, talking and drinking late into the night. Though much of our conversation surrounded some of our most recent decisions—our marriages, careers, and motherhood—we did slip back into the years we spent in college. Because they were both RAs, much of their experience surrounded the time they shared with the other RAs, counseling freshmen, spring break vacations, parties, and float trips. In that moment in the bar, listening to them recount their experiences, I realized something I never knew before:

My RA enjoyed the hell out of college.

CHOOSING MEANS *ASKING*

The phrase I use most with my daughters is, "Use your words." Also, I say, "*I'm* the boss, not *you!*" but that's to be expected with strong-willed girls. Anyway, forcing children to verbalize what they want is a powerful lesson. But we kind of slack off when they become surly teenagers, and then people forget how to use their words.

Frank Flynn, a professor of organizational behavior at Stanford University, researched the concept of asking for what we need and want. In his study, participants were first asked to estimate how many strangers would help them if asked to provide a favor. Then participants had to carry out those asks. Favors varied from asking to use a cell phone to asking people to fill out surveys, and a variety of small requests in between. This process was repeated with larger groups of people—and later modified with asking for donations rather than favors—and the results were the same. Those asking for help grossly underestimated how willing strangers would be to help. The researchers said this is in part because of the social pressure to help—otherwise you look like a jackass. But another part of it is that when we need or want something, whether we're asking for help or for what we want in life, we believe we are going to be denied.

This concept gets played out in a variety of ways, such as with the mom who does too much but is afraid to ask her spouse for help, or the manager who has too much responsibility and is afraid to delegate, or the job candidate afraid to negotiate salary. Yet our ability to get what we want (out of life, love, work, and home) almost *always* relies on the aid of others. So, say what you want and ask for what you need. You want to get ahead? You're going to need some support. No matter if you are going up for a promotion, going back to school, or trying to win a hot dog eating contest, you are going to need to ask for help along the way and make it clear to others what it is you are going after and why. And when things aren't going the way you need them to go, you must ask for a change.

One semester I began receiving complaints about an assignment that was given in another professor's class. I fielded emails, phone calls, and office visits from people upset by the amount of time the assignment was taking. Each student who talked to me would explain their concerns in detail. I would validate their frustration and encourage them to tell their professor. Over and over, I urged the students to talk directly with the instructor. After the twelfth student stopped by to ask about dropping the course, I began to realize something: A choice had been made, but no one was asking.

Finally, one student felt empowered enough by my encouragement to email the professor. She explained that the class was distraught by what seemed like a cruel and unusual assignment. She begged the instructor to grade on a curve and reconsider all future assignments.

The next morning, the professor knocked on my door. "So, have you heard my entire class is beside themselves over my last assignment?" I nodded. "Why did they wait until *after* they turned it in to tell me their concerns?"

Sometimes it's hard to speak up, especially to someone in a position of authority. Some students found comfort in coming to me—as someone who wasn't in power in this situation—rather than the one assigning the grades. But once the instructor was made aware of the issue, she made fair adjustments. A few weeks after the incident, I stopped by her office to check in. When I inquired about the students, she said, "I thought about their feedback and agreed with a lot of it. So I allowed for an extension on the assignment and I reduced the number of questions on the next assignment. All they had to do was ask."

If you ever find yourself in a position like those students—in which you've determined the problem, developed an opinion, and identified a solution—remember that you still have to use your words.

And on that, let's talk for just a minute about negotiating for your salary. The wage gap between women and men is real and unfortunate. It rests in the hands of industries and policy to correct that. But there's also something women can do: negotiate. Carnegie Melon University conducted a study a decade ago about salary negotiations and found that only 7 percent of women negotiated, while nearly 60 percent of men did. Fortunately, that gap is closing slightly in the eighteen-to-twenty-four age bracket. The most recent data on the topic, from San Francisco lending company Ernest, found that in that age range, about 27 percent of women negotiated, compared to 44 percent of men. But still, women—for a variety of reasons—hesitate to negotiate salary.

When I was offered my first job out of college, I responded, "You bet!" to the organization's first offer. Two months later they hired a guy my age in a similar position. After he'd been on the job a few weeks, the executive director called me into her office and said, "Meg, we hired David at $5,000 more a year than we hired you." My brow furrowed as I tried to understand why she was telling me this. "It's not that we offered him more; he *asked* for more." I stared on in confusion. She continued: "So what I'm going to do is raise your salary to meet his if you promise me one thing." I nodded slowly. "Never, ever, let that happen again."

A dozen years later, I've made it a mission to help my female students negotiate their starting salaries. Among the numerous examples I've seen of their successful negotiations, two are especially enlightening.

The first was a student who was offered a job that represented a career shift for her. Instead of assuming she should take lower pay just because she was newer to the field, she countered back with 5 percent higher than the initial offer. Guess what? She got the extra money. On her first day on the job, her boss came to her office and said, "In all my years hiring people, you're the first woman who ever negotiated her salary." As my student recounted this story, she marveled at the simplicity of the transaction. "All it took was one email and I got what I wanted," she said.

The second example involved a student who was desperate to get out of her current job, so she quickly accepted a lower offer at another organization. When she told me about it, I asked why she was willing to take a new job for less money. She offered up all kinds of reasons: she was desperate to leave her old job; she didn't have much experience; she was afraid she'd look greedy. When I encouraged her to go back and counter for a bit more, she said it was too late; she had already signed the offer letter. I shrugged and said, "You haven't even started the job." Feeling remorseful for rationalizing a low salary just out of desperation, she finally agreed to ask. She drafted an email and sent it to the hiring manager, who wrote back to say, "Since you've already signed the letter, there's not much I can do. But I'll try." My student was panicked—concerned she looked greedy—and asked whether she should just write back and say, "Never mind!" I urged her to remain strong and wait until they responded. Sure enough, two days later the company came back and met her requests.

The point is: Ask for what you want. And if for some reason you didn't ask for what you wanted in the moment, understand that it's never too late to reopen negotiations.

• • •

There is a sound machine in every bedroom of our house, and I leave them turned on at pleasing levels all day, every day. When Lowery was a newborn, I had hers turned on to the "heartbeat" setting. After eight weeks, she burst out of her swaddle sack and tried to pull up the floorboards.

So I switched the setting to "downpour" and there it stayed. In our bedroom, the sound machine has always been set to "ocean." Before London was born, our house was just one long, rainy day at the beach.

But as I was preparing for our second child, I had to decide which noise machine would be best for the new baby. I didn't find frogs of the Amazon to be all that soothing, and thunder could potentially be frightening. The hoot owl was a bit too ominous, and the lullaby setting would most certainly spark an anxiety attack in me. I opted for a simple "white noise" machine. The package promised to create a restful environment for the baby, assured me she'd get a good night's sleep, and guaranteed to lower the age of potty training.

On the first night home from the hospital with London, I flicked on the noise machine, filling the nursery with a gentle, whirring hum. It stayed on around the clock for the next two years and two months.

Until recently.

I had done the usual routine for London's bedtime: giving her a bath; brushing her teeth; coaxing her off the stool she stands on to brush her teeth; reading her a book; singing her a song; and placing her into the crib, sleepy and happy.

Back downstairs, not a few minutes later, I heard London call out:

"Mommy, what's that noise?"

I waited a moment or two to see if she could answer her own question—the tell-tale sign of parenting the second time around—but she kept calling out, demanding to know what the noise was.

I begrudgingly climbed back up the stairs to her room, only to hear nothing. But she was standing, covering her ears, and screaming for the noise to stop. I looked around the room to locate the source of the sound. I ran out into the hallway and across to the bathroom to make sure the water had been turned off at the sink. But there was no noise. The air conditioner wasn't even running. All I could hear was the peaceful white noise drifting from the miracle machine in the corner.

"Do you mean this?" I asked as I flipped the sound machine off.

London visibly relaxed, her cupped hands dropping from the sides of her head. She nodded enthusiastically.

"But Lunny, this is your noise machine. You have slept with it on every night for two years." I flicked it back on.

"No!" she yelled. "I don't want that noise! No more noise! Turn it off!"

And in deference to that rare outburst from my youngest, I flipped off the machine and walked out. She quickly fell asleep.

London's ability to ask for exactly what she wants, and nothing more, is one of her most defining characteristics. Her sister, Lowery, is the kind who asks for everything she wants, plus a bit more in case she wants it later, and a bit of something else on the chance she changes her mind about the first thing she asked for. Then she'll ask why you aren't getting all those things for her right this second. She'll also ask why you seem so irritated.

But London uses her asks in a different way. She's more methodical and a bit more forceful. When she was just over a year old, we discovered London had an extreme aversion to elevators, causing her to fall into an emotional pit of despair every time we visited the pediatrician. Given that it was one of very few quirks, we happily climbed several flights of stairs to keep her happy. That's something we'd never do for her sister because Lowery would have as big an opinion about the stairwell as she would about the elevator. But then, a year later, London insisted on elevators again, forgetting all the panic-induced screaming she'd done in the past.

For the past few years, I've thought my husband and I always let London have what she wanted when she asked for it because she asked for so much less than Lowery. Then we theorized it was because she was the second born and this was a common birth order default. Or maybe our concessions were sheer laziness. Later we hypothesized that it equaled out because they both got the same amount, it's just that Lowery got less than she asked for and London got more. Finally, we agreed that we were—as usual—overthinking it, so we threw a bunch of cookies at both girls and lay down for a nap.

No matter how much we give in or stand strong—and obsess why and when we do either—someone is *always* asking for something.

There is so much asking, begging, pleading, demanding, and whining that I'm not sure my children know how to speak sentences without their voices going up at the end to make it a question. On one end is Lowery, asking for everything. On the other is London, holding out for bigger asks.

Addressing all their demands has not just made me a fairly irritated person, it has also taught me the power of asking. At home I've utilized the Lowery method of asking by demanding the children do a lot of things for me. For example, I now ask that they take their dinner plates to the sink (though sometimes they land on the floor); I ask that they clean their rooms (though they technically leave them messier); I ask that they let me pee alone (though they think talking to me through the bathroom door is a good compromise). But I just keep on asking. The odds are, I'll get something I ask for.

And I've embraced the London method of reverse asking, by changing my mind about what I want any damn time I please. For example, I never minded where the girls did their coloring, but then recently changed my mind, only allowing it at the kitchen table (they were coloring a little too far outside the lines). I previously insisted they always had either Jim or me outside with them while they played, but then later both of us refused to go outside with them (that's Oklahoma in the summer for you). I once promised them I would read any book they brought to me at any time, citing the importance of reading, but later changed my policy to exclude a few choice titles (*Clifford the Big Red Dog; Green Eggs and Ham*).

I've also adapted the girls' approaches into my professional life. Having just wrapped up another semester,

I'm aware I asked a lot of the students. They read two entire books and more than thirty-five peer-reviewed journal articles, wrote seven papers, and prepared and delivered a presentation, all in the span of three weekends. This isn't uncommon. That's an acceptable workload for a graduate student (I mean don't ask them, they are still tired and cranky), but I recognize that even though it's acceptable, it's still asking a lot. It's asking them to give up three weekends to come to campus and sit, in fluorescent lighting and brutally cold air conditioning, while we collectively work through all the course material. It's asking them to be away from their families, give up activities, and miss out on sunshine. On top of all those asks, I keep making even more asks. Notably, I ask for no cell phones or laptops during class. Of all the things I ask for, that might be the biggest.

I ask for all of this in every class I teach. Happily for me, everyone always complies. And this summer I had yet another ask, one I had never made before because I was fully aware of all the other asks I was making of them: I asked that they obey my new policy of no late papers. Now, this seems like an obvious one—get your assignments in on time. But with graduate school, it's not always that easy. All the students have full-time jobs with a great amount of responsibility. Many are married and some have kids. A handful are commuting long distances to attend class. For those reasons, my policy has always been that late papers will be accepted (typically for points deducted) on a case-by-case, better-have-a-damn-good-excuse basis.

But, for the first time in ten years of teaching, I decided I wasn't going to allow late assignments. As I drafted the syllabus in late spring, I realized how much I was looking forward to the summer break. The more time I spent grading, the less time I would be able to spend doing regular summer activities in Oklahoma, like taking pictures of the thermometer on my dashboard. Delayed assignment submissions inhibit my ability to finish grading, or at least draw it out into times I'd rather be doing anything else.

Surprisingly, not a single student complained about my new ask, even those who had taken four or five courses with me and had benefited from the occasional extended deadline. I wasn't exactly expecting a coup, but I was expecting more pushback. Yet the class went as smoothly as ever, and every assignment was turned in on time. By every single student. And aside from the group collectively trying to delay deadlines in jest, no one privately asked for an extension.

I guess my hesitation in making the ask was only because I was worried I had asked for too much already, and that it was too late to make an ask that was such a departure from what I'd previously allowed.

But Lowery demonstrated that was ridiculous, showing me I can ask for every damn thing I want and then some, for good measure. And London reinforced how perfectly acceptable it is to change my mind and make asks that accommodate.

Despite it all, asking for what I really want—what I really *need*—is difficult, maybe because there is always potential to not get what I want. But then I remember, that never stops Lowery. She just keeps on asking and asking and asking, even when I ask her to stop asking. And I think of London, who realigns her asks when her needs change. I've learned that the right time to ask for more, or to ask for a change, is the exact moment I feel I need it. I may have begged for the noise, but it's also okay to ask for silence.

• • •

Choice is the path to your wants. That might make choices more overwhelming to you, but it shouldn't be- cause wants are big and choices are small. Wants can of- ten feel immovable within you, but choices are nimble. Choices are the tiny steps up the huge mountain of want. Most of your choices are small enough that they only inch you closer, but if they inch you a bit further away, it's easy to correct. Be excited by choices. And, perhaps most im- portant of all, when you've made your choices, do yourself a favor and stick with them.

Even when I encourage my kids (and my students) to use their words, they often still have moments of in- security about their choices. My older daughter will use her words to such volume and quantity that it's very clear she wants a bowl of cereal, in the blue bowl, with lots of milk, and the Mickey Mouse spoon. And she'll sit happily at the table having made all her choices, asked for what she wanted, and succeeded at getting it all. But then her younger sister will wander into the kitchen and ask for a peanut butter sandwich and, suddenly, the older child is fraught with remorse.

Sticking by our choices is tough, and it's easy to want to abandon them when we see other options float by. That's a normal feeling. It's also just insecurity. We doubt our own ability to choose. We doubt for a number of reasons, some of which may or may not be grounded in our relationships with our mothers. But, regardless, own your choices, not just to be stubborn or to appear overly confident, but because you made that choice for a reason. Sure, you are going to make bad choices, and your choices will be tested. But make sure you respect yourself and your choices enough to give them time.

The Closer
for TACTIC TWO

- **Understand** that when choices are made for you, more choices open up.

- **Recognize** that the biggest choice you have to make is how to react.

- **Acknowledge** that your relationships are your choice.

- **Accept** that no single choice will satisfy you.

- **Appreciate** when and why you get into a cycle of choice.

- **Remember** that choosing isn't official until you *ask* for what you've chosen.

OWNING

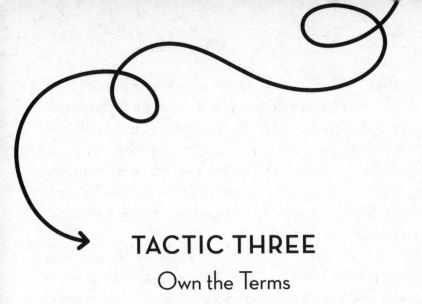

TACTIC THREE
Own the Terms

A major part of my professional role is helping graduate students navigate job placement or promotion. I am either on the phone with a potential employer providing a reference, meeting one-on-one with a student to run mock interviews, or helping that same student negotiate for their starting salary. In general, I'm helping students be bold in their quest for a satisfying career that will pay them what they deserve.

There have also been times, however, when I'm the one doing the hiring. Sometimes I'm conducting interviews for my own graduate research assistant positions, or I'm serving on hiring committees for other faculty members or some select staff members at our university. But the biggest hire I ever made was for a CEO of a highly visible, local nonprofit. Given my leadership position on the board—at the time I was the incoming president—coupled with my academic knowledge of nonprofit management, I co-chaired the search committee for the CEO of an organization that serves women, immigrants, and refugees; has about 100 employees; provides services to thousands in the community; and operates on a multimillion dollar budget.

I spent nearly an entire summer, while on break from my teaching and academic duties, assembling a strong and diverse search committee, combing through resumes, conducting phone screens, holding multiple rounds of interviews, and checking references. This undertaking was overwhelming, and I took it seriously.

Though we ultimately found a wonderful candidate who has since gone on to do great and transformative things for the organization, the search for her took several months, during which I was reminded of a few things I've impressed upon my students.

Most notably, when it comes to getting what you want—such as a CEO position—*you* are the thing that stands between getting the job and not. Not your degree, not your experience with X or Y, not your current job, and not the awards section on your resume. You.

This isn't to say your experience and credentials don't matter. But your experience and credentials just get you in the game; they don't win it for you. There's a lot of rhetoric suggesting the whole hiring process favors those who are simply good in interviews, and I can certainly see some truth in that after interviewing dozens of candidates over several months. We had applicants who weren't an ideal fit on paper, but they did a bang-up job convincing us in the interview. And there were those who seemed qualified on paper, but somehow convinced us in the interview that they weren't. It wasn't enough to be qualified. The candidates who made it to the final round were qualified, but it was their skill in articulating their qualifications (especially if they didn't exactly match what we were asking for) that sealed the deal.

You see, the committee members had some qualities in mind that we wanted. After consulting with the board of directors, the staff, and a few key donors, we spent weeks working on a list of qualifications. But what we came up with in the job description was a wish list. They are always just a wish list! We knew we weren't going to find someone with all those qualifications. The famous Hewlett Packard report (as cited in *Lean In*) shows how women applied only for jobs for which they thought they were 100 percent qualified, while men would apply to jobs for which they were only 60 percent qualified. This finding played out in our applicant pool.

While we did get numerous strong and varied applicants, we also had to do some recruiting to get more *women* to apply—to lead a women's organization! We made a few calls to some known and highly qualified candidates who told us on the phone, "I'm not sure I'm qualified for such a role." Meanwhile, we had the application of a twenty-three-year-old man who was the manager of a local Long John Silver's. We needed a strong pool of diverse candidates to lead this social justice organization boldly, but we had to convince a few of our candidates they were even qualified. Imagine if we hadn't known about and accommodated this invisible obstacle women put in front of themselves. We might currently be serving local women and immigrants with a side of hush puppies.

We needed to find someone with *some* of the qualifications and the ability to explain how they could compensate for any of those they didn't have from our wish list. Those candidates who *owned* the process made it to the top. They took ownership of their capabilities, applied, walked in, and then took every minute of their time with the committee to shape their narrative. Those who moved ahead in the process didn't hide their crisscross career trajectory, but rather owned it, made it make sense, and expressed what a variety of skills they gathered along the way.

The point is this: Own it. Own your abilities and your narrative around those abilities. Own everything you can, even your weaknesses. Qualifications matter, but only to a point. *You* own and set the terms. Your ability to go far and get what you want rests largely on your own belief in yourself and your ability to sell that belief to others. I cannot stress this enough. But allow me to try.

OWN YOUR NARRATIVE

Owning your narrative means controlling the messaging around who you are, what you stand for, and what you deserve. This is tough to do, particularly for women. Women don't like to talk about themselves. I can even say that despite being an outgoing and talkative person,

I hate to talk about myself. This scenario plays out most noticeably at the beginning of every semester on the first day of class. I always have students introduce themselves, talk about where they work and why they are in the program, and answer some sort of get-to-know-you prompt, like a book they would recommend or what famous person they would most like to meet. Once every student has spoken, it's my turn to more fully introduce myself. And while I should talk about my role at the university, the research I'm interested in, my teaching philosophy, and a little about myself (I'll go with *Bossypants* and Tina Fey), I always rush past this part with a condensed introduction that goes something like, "I'm Dr. Morgan, this is the classroom, this is the textbook, this here is my pen; let's get started." To their credit, the students always ask follow-up questions, but it's the one portion of the class I'm always eager to move past. During lectures and discussions, they can't shut me up. Why is this?

A researcher at Yale University, Corinne Moss-Racusin, studied how women talk about themselves; or, more to the point, how they brag about themselves. Her conclusion was essentially that we don't. She gathered a group of male and female participants for a mock interview. The interview questions asked participants to talk about successes they've had in their career—in other words, to brag about themselves. Moss-Racusin found that while men were quick to take credit, women were quick to give credit to others, perhaps other members on their team. Not only that, but when women *do* brag, they are judged way more harshly.

I found this played out while we were interviewing candidates for the CEO role. One male candidate was quick to take credit for a variety of initiatives in his current role. When pressed on one particular Herculean feat, he said, "Well, to be fair, it was my wife's idea, and my team implemented it. But I supplied the resources." There's nothing wrong with this, of course; leadership is about recognizing great ideas and delegating them for execution. But we had to keep probing a few of our female candidates to talk more about what they'd accomplished—we needed to know specifically what they had done, and for some candidates, this was tough. One even said, "I really hate bragging, but…"

Talking about ourselves or taking credit for our hard work is just a small piece of owning our narrative. It's the part of our narrative other people see and hear. But a bigger part of owning our narrative is getting clear on the story we tell ourselves.

• • •

My office hours are filled with stories, mostly from my female students as they stop by to chat. Sometimes I get to hear the story of a new puppy or a promotion at work; sometimes it's a darker tale I feel humbled to hear. I am surrounded by the presence of women and their stories, and I've noticed that often, we don't do the best job as storytellers. I find women spend the least amount of time crafting their own stories. I see them getting swept up in other people's narratives, playing a secondary character in someone else's tale, or—even worse—giving up on their own stories. But if you see your life as a story, you can use three rules of storytelling to weave a tale you are proud to tell—to yourself and to others.

1. Don't Just Be the Hero

I constantly hear the phrase, *Be the hero of your own story.* I see it on posters, on memes, on home décor. And that is fine advice. We *should* be the hero of our own story. But I've seen enough Disney movies with my daughters to know that even when the princess is the hero of the story, it's always narrated by someone else, an omnipresent voice telling us the hero's journey and, often, how to feel about it. It's not enough to be the hero of your story. Be the narrator. Then, write it with you as the hero.

Remember earlier when I said that pursuing school and having kids at the same time had positive outcomes? Well, before I could get to those positive outcomes, I had to first get my narrative. I had lost control of it for a while. It was after the birth of my first daughter, and I was in the middle of my doctoral degree. I was able to secure two days of childcare. This meant that on Tuesdays and Thursdays I would need to attend class, do any of the university work to fulfill my scholarship requirements, and schedule any dentist or doctor appointments. On Mondays, Wednesdays, and Fridays I was with my newborn, taking her to story time at the library, Mommy and Me gymnastics class, or to see the elephants at the zoo. I worked on my dissertation while she napped. When Jim came home from work, I made us dinner and then left to drive an hour away to another university, where I taught two night classes that lasted until about 11:00 p.m. The next morning, it started all over again. This was my routine for two years.

At the time, when people would ask what I was doing now that the baby had arrived, I enumerated all of that. And almost every person I told this to responded in one of three ways: 1) gasp and express how lucky I was to find a man who would support me in all of this; 2) bring up the financial ramifications of my choices; many were quick to point out that the expense of graduate school must have put undue pressure on Jim to support us fully on his salary; or 3) lightly suggest that I could be on the verge of ruining all of it.

The narrative was: Here's a woman being careless, selfish, and irresponsible with her family. And after frequently hearing that story told about my own life, I bought into that narrative so completely that it became the story I believed and told, too. I'd sheepishly say I was in school, but express that it wasn't a big deal. Or I'd lead by saying how lucky I was to have a husband like Jim who supported my schoolwork. Or I'd undersell how overwhelmed I was because I didn't want anyone assuming my stress meant stress in our marriage.

One morning in the shower, while scrubbing my hair, I enumerated all I had to do that day: get Jim off to work, feed and change the baby, get her to daycare, get to class, go into the office to run data for the grant I was working on, get my hair cut, pick up the baby, get dinner ready, grade papers while we ate, and create my lecture in my head while I drove an hour to class. And it suddenly hit me: The narrative was all wrong.

The true story was this: I was and am lucky to have Jim, but not for the reasons people kept saying. If the rationale is that I am lucky because my spouse supports me in my personal and professional goals, then Jim is lucky, too. I supported him every bit as much as he supported me. I was also not a financial burden at all. I was caring for our child nearly full time (saving us thousands of dollars), I was on full scholarship for school (again, several thousands of dollars), and I was bringing in money from adjunct teaching (let's not split hairs here). Further, I wasn't on the verge of ruining my marriage with all my stress. I handle stress well. And it was insulting to imply I wouldn't be aware of it if I were.

Wasn't any of my journey impressive? Wasn't anything I was doing worthy of admiration or respect? Why was it that everyone saw my story only as it related to my seemingly poor, put-upon, stressed out, financially struggling husband? How had he become the hero of my story? It was because I had let go of the narrative. Well, that and because society is an expert at placing disproportionate expectations on women. Yeah, society had my narrative, too.

After that shower, when I was good and steamed, I took back my narrative, sometimes in overt ways—like writing about it—but often just in how I responded to people who asked about my life. I stopped downplaying it or hiding it, for fear I would seem selfish and reckless. I was proud of my story, and I took pride in the narrative. I reveled in my story because I realized I was the hero.

I see a lot of women who let their narratives go to someone else, be it a parent, a child, a spouse, or even strangers. The problem with that is that no one else is ever going to write you as the hero.

Recently, a young woman who had just graduated college asked to meet with me. She was interested in applying to the graduate program I administer. She told me that she wanted to do the program, she just didn't know when. Her problem was she was waiting to see where her boyfriend got a job. Then she would probably move with him because they were probably going to get married and then she could make a decision about starting graduate school.

I have no problem with women embarking on an adventure for love. But in that conversation, she was talking more about her boyfriend's career, opportunities, and desires than her own. She had given him the narrative and was living as a secondary character in his story. And if she gave over the narrative that time, making the boyfriend the hero, she's more likely to do it again. And again.

Life is about compromise, but that doesn't mean giving over your narrative. Be the hero of your own story. More important, be the one telling your story. And dare to write yourself as heroically as you can.

2. Don't Put Plot Before Character

The most interesting and compelling stories are made up of characters you can relate to, fall in love with, and root for. The stuff that happens to them is just plot, and it only matters because of who the character is. If you ask someone about *Harry Potter*, they don't say, "Oh, I love all that stuff that happens to Harry Potter." No, they say, "I love Harry Potter." At that point, it's best to walk away because they are about to tell you all the many reasons why they do, and you do not have that kind of time.

I find that people—especially women—focus on the plot way more than the character.

I met with a prospective student one summer. I knew her only by her sterling reputation, so I was beyond excited when she reached out to me about the graduate program. She started our meeting with a disclaimer that she was going to have a baby. I was thrilled for this stranger, congratulating her for the good news. She promptly corrected me by saying she wasn't actually pregnant yet, but she wanted me to know her frame of mind to give our conversation context.

This isn't unusual. Many of the women I talk to mention this up front. I think it's great to voice our desires. As their potential advisor, it helps me know what kind of life they are striving for—which is helpful when it comes to career counseling and course selection.

But the reason for mentioning her interest in having a child was because she couldn't decide whether she wanted to take the program I administer—which is a traditional in-person program—or one offered at another university online.

Again, that isn't an unusual conflict, and I've heard many potential students express it. She thought that an online degree would offer more flexibility, which would be helpful whenever a child arrived. There's a lot of data that suggests online programs are actually more time-consuming, but I could tell that wasn't the direction our conversation needed to go, or the real root of her dilemma. So I asked her, "Which one do you *want* to do?"

She laughed and said she would much rather take the program in person. She loved having conversations with her classmates, getting to interact with the professors, the camaraderie of school, and so forth.

Her conflict wasn't between an online program and a traditional one. Her conflict was between plot (the kid) and character (the in-person class). She clearly had a preference. And the reality was, her preference wasn't detrimental to her other plot points—her future kid won't know the difference. But women continually jump to the plot point before they've thought about the character.

One of the biggest fallacies women believe is that plot governs character. They believe that the major plot point of parenting is immediate sacrifice, so they start sacrificing before they are ever asked to. I'm not saying parenting doesn't come with some sacrifice; it does. And you never know what issues or challenges will come with each child. But by and large, my kids aren't the ones asking me to sacrifice. The sacrifice my daughters ask me to make is to get off the couch and get them Goldfish crackers, not to give up on my hopes and dreams.

Yet when women are ready for motherhood, they start clearing their lives of all the things they really want in preparation for all the sacrificing.

If we think about character first, then logical plot lines flow from there. The prospective student can choose to do the program she wants and make the arrangements with the baby around that. But if she jumps to plot first, picking a program she is less excited about just because she thinks the plot dictates that, then she is not only putting plot before character, but she's handing over her narrative to a person who doesn't even exist yet.

So, if you've got a hold of your narrative, and you're writing yourself as the hero, then accept the plot points that make sense from the point of view of your main character. Which is you. Remember? The hero.

3. Don't Recycle Plot Lines

My husband and I stream a lot of Netflix, Hulu, and Amazon Prime. We've instituted two minutes of uninterrupted eye contact between episodes, so it's fine. Sometimes, a few minutes into a new show, we'll turn to each other and say, "Have we seen this? This seems familiar." Now, whether or not we have actually seen it before, the seeming familiarity has already weakened our interest.

Our own plot lines should be compelling and unique and keep us on the edge of our seats as we progress in the story. If it feels familiar, you're going to be bored. And yet we often get caught up in the common plot points we've heard about. I'm not talking about big major life milestones, like school, marriage, kids, and the like. I'm talking about the small points of plot we think are necessary for our character to experience.

For the first two years recruiting for our graduate program I got the exact same question from every prospective student: "What can I do with this degree?" For two years

I showed them statistics on what other students had gone on to do. I showed them income reporting from alumni across the region. I showed them the most common jobs that look for someone with this degree. But after two years, I had a young woman in my office who asked that same question and I snapped (I apologized, we're good) and said, "What *can't* you do with this degree?" I was just so tired of recycling plot lines to students.

I get that people don't want to take unnecessary risks. But there's also a point at which we must stop thinking that if we follow the same path as someone else, it will lead to the same outcome. Or that we can only get to point B if we go through point A. I'm guessing going through Z is way more fun anyway. Very few things in life have a replication model of success. There is no direct path to anything.

But I see my students, especially my female students, get caught up in the tiniest points of plot when they don't follow the prescribed order. I recently had a student in my office who was upset that she wasn't going to be able to fulfill the requirements in our program for a "concentration," which is three courses in a specialized area. She bemoaned the fact that she hadn't realized there was a concentration option until she had already taken all of her electives. She was worried this would impact her success on the job market.

I explained to her that there won't be a hiring manager who has her resume sitting next to someone else's *identical* resume, and one more line of a concentration on that other resume will be the deciding factor. I reminded her that she is more than just tiny plot points that other people have already experienced (concentrations, degrees, trainings). She's a character, and a narrator. And she can easily get into an interview and tell her own story of why she's the best candidate. Very rarely, if ever, does a transcript or a resume do that.

Don't get swept up in recycled plot points. They are simply experiences other people have used in their story. And if you insist they must be in your story, you're going to get that sinking feeling of familiarity that causes people to stop streaming.

The story of your life can be as dramatic, mysterious, romantic, adventurous, or funny as you choose to make it. You own your story. You pick the plot points; you choose the cast of characters. And while you are in the middle of composing your story, remember how little it matters how anyone else perceives it. Don't worry about what others think of your choices or your life. You can only write your story; you can't tell others how to read it. The only thing standing between you and a great story is simply your own ability to narrate it.

So tell it well.

FIND YOUR OWN VOICE

Owning our narrative means being in charge of our story, telling our side of things, crafting our message, narrating our destiny. But beyond that, we have to find our voice in day-to-day life. More simply put, we must speak the hell up.

I pride myself on the classroom dynamics I've been able to orchestrate. My classes are always discussion-based and are usually solid three-hour blocks of spitfire debate, with everyone chiming in with their counter to each argument. This approach became such a hallmark of my classes that I sometimes forgot it was harder for some students than others. There are some students who are naturally going to sit at the back and be quieter. They are not punished for this. They speak only occasionally—it's usually mind-blowing—and then they go back to doodling quietly in their notebook. But one day, several weeks into the semester, Lynn came up to me after class. She was new and quiet, and she spoke so softly I could barely hear her voice.

"I'm terrified to speak up," she muttered. I nodded and assured her that was okay, she was fine to sit there and just take it all in—she wouldn't be counted down for not speaking up.

"But I have so much to say," she mumbled.

"How can I help during the discussion?" I asked. "It's not my style to call students out, but would you want to nod at me when you have something to say so I can bring you into the fold?"

She shook her head and asked me to just give her time. A few weeks later she emailed me to say again how terrified she was to speak up. When I emailed back I asked, "What is the worst thing that will happen?" She responded, "That I'll sound stupid." This, by the way, is the biggest gender divide I've noticed in all my years teaching: Men are concerned about being heard (they even talk louder when they speak in class); women are worried about how they will be perceived (so they sometimes won't talk at all).

Lynn never did get the courage to speak up in class, but she got in the habit of emailing after every class to tell me the thoughts she was too afraid to voice. These emails were lengthy, thoughtful, and provoking. But what could I do with them? Forward them on to the entire class and say, "See? She is so smart but too afraid you'll think she's not!" Or follow her into the workforce and read her emails after every meeting in which she refused to talk? The thing of it was, she *is* smart and has something to say, but it means nothing if she doesn't speak up. This is why I've always hated the quote, "Better to be quiet and thought a fool than to speak and remove all doubt." The quote really should be, "You can remain voiceless and still be thought a fool, so why not just speak the hell up because you've got nothing to lose!" Stitch *that* on a pillow.

I've had plenty of students ask for tips on how to speak up in class, and not one of them has been a man. If anything, I've had to work hard to get the men in the classroom to pipe down so the women can be heard. This isn't just what happens in the classroom, of course; speaking up as a woman is often a huge roadblock at work no matter the profession. Research points to the idea that women struggle to speak up, especially in meetings.

A 2012 study from Harvard looked at thousands of women in executive-level positions (so, not even the lower-level employees who might already feel voiceless) to gauge what their stumbling blocks were in their job.

Being able to speak up and feeling heard was one of the top concerns. Their male counterparts perceived the female executives as lacking confidence, and in turn, the women noted feeling a lack of confidence to be able to speak up in meetings. Damn this cycle!

In most every class I teach, students prepare and deliver a group presentation. During a recent class, one group was made up of four women and one man. Purely by the organization of their presentation, the man spoke last. For the first ten minutes, the three women took turns talking. While I could hear what they were saying, I noticed I was leaning forward in my chair. When I looked around, I saw that, similarly, almost every student in the class was leaned slightly forward to hear better. When it was time for the man to speak, his voice was so much louder and clearer—though he was not by any means shouting—that I saw a group of thirty students collectively lean back in their chairs and relax. The group did outstanding work on their research and assembled (and rehearsed) a professional presentation. But in the end, the male voice was the most distinct, and only because he truly projected.

The point is, you gotta speak up. When your friends say, "What should we do tonight?" or a boss says, "Anyone have any other great ideas?" you have to be a voice that's heard. When you talk, make sure you speak up so others can truly hear you. Your voice says a lot about your confidence, your competence, and your trust in others. Don't take your voice for granted. If you've made it to the table—or the front of the classroom, or the center of the stage—don't let your voice be taken from you.

• • •

When I was in high school there was a song that hit it big. Well, it wasn't a song so much as a commencement speech spoken over a catchy beat. The speech/song, "Free to Wear Sunscreen," topped the charts in the spring, and I think that year's graduating class at my high school even used it for their own commencement, which at the time seemed super hip and fresh, but looking back now I can see it was actually kind of lazy.

Regardless, the speech was set to music and released on an album by filmmaker Baz Luhrmann. He is probably best known for directing *Romeo + Juliet*, starring Leo DiCaprio and Claire Danes. Most girls I went to school with truly lost their shit over this movie. And, as a result, I had to fake the loss of my own shit, despite hating the movie, because that's how peer pressure works.

At the time, "Free to Wear Sunscreen" was known as that commencement speech the irreverent Kurt Vonnegut gave to graduates of the Massachusetts Institute of Technology. That fact intrigued me the most, as I was a very progressive and heady teenager who was into all things Vonnegut. This made me highly intelligent and, also, a bit too cool for school.

The speech gives sound advice. Not just most notably to "wear sunscreen," but also unforgettable lines like,

"Don't waste your time on jealousy. Sometimes you're ahead, sometimes you're behind. The race is long and, in the end, it's only with yourself." As a teenager who was prone to beat myself up too much, I needed this advice.

And while the quote spoke to me at the time—as a young, tie-dye-wearing, misunderstood Vonnegut lover—it resonated even more on the way home from work one day, when I heard it spoken by Baz on the radio for the first time in more than fifteen years.

In my beginning years of teaching at the college level, I unknowingly developed a bad habit: I favored the male students. While this was completely unintentional, I came to the realization a few years in that I was constantly deferring to the men in my classes. In my flimsy defense, there were many reasons why this was the case. For starters, during my first five years, I was an adjunct teaching undergrads at night in a different town. Often, I was the only person in the entire building late at night with my thirty or so students. To some degree, both conscious and unconscious, I felt a bit of fear as a young woman with so many male students. One night in class, during a particularly heated debate about gun control in which two male students became verbally threatening, I had justification.

Aside from that, I've always gotten along well with men. In the romantic comedy of life, I am continually typecast as the protagonist's funny best friend. I was a friend to boys growing up. I was a friend to boys in college. And I worked better with men than with women in my first few jobs. So, as an instructor, I naturally gave men the attention I'd always given them. All of that is on me.

But, the other side is that the men naturally behaved differently in class. They talked louder, interjected without fear, effortlessly criticized my thoughts or those of their classmates, blurted out without thought, and never struggled to speak their minds. This is an intimidating and powerful thing to watch from the perspective of the instructor. No wonder I favored them; they gave me something to favor.

And yet, the women in my class were consistently better writers, more effective public speakers, more thoughtful debaters, and kinder classmates. So when it finally occurred to me, on the long drive home one night after class, that I was more likely to pay attention to the men—because of fear, intimidation, interest, and awe—I knew I had to change my ways.

I publicly apologized to the students at the next class. I spoke to everyone but only made eye contact with the women. I said that while I knew I had been fair in grading, perhaps I'd been too quick to defer to the louder, deeper voices in the class. And, from that day forward, I pledged to be the biggest advocate the women in the class ever had. I offered private meetings, reference letters, job counseling, or a copy of *Bossypants*. And then I challenged them to speak up, sit in the front row, interject more, and not be overrun by the male voices in the class as I had been.

Everyone stared at me blankly.

After class that night, I felt foolish. How arrogant of me to assume any of the female students needed my advice, let alone wanted it. Maybe my favoritism toward the men had been invisible to them. Did I just draw their attention to something they'd never even noticed? Did I offend the women? Alienate the men? The next day I received two emails, both from female students, both asking for letters of recommendation. A third asked for career advice, and a handful of others started following me on social media.

Currently—having moved on from long commutes and late-night classes to a full-time position with office hours—I find myself in very different terrain. My relationships with my female students are different. For one thing, women don't struggle in class to compete with the men; they contribute equally. I don't find myself deferring to the male voices, as they typically never overpower a woman's. Happily, my female and male students are equal in the classroom. Both genders interject without fear and challenge each other. Both are strong writers, good speakers, and kind to each other.

But as a faculty member, I find myself in meetings in which I'm one of few women. Despite trying hard to never come across as rude or pushy, I've been shut down by men in meetings. I would physically shrink myself in my chair next to these men, ashamed I was allowing them to get to me.

In one meeting, several of us were there to talk to one highly positioned woman, who held valuable information we all needed. She was, without a doubt, the only reason a group of men (and myself) were assembled in a room; we were there to hear what she had to say. As the meeting started, she began freely sharing the knowledge we were there to absorb. When she paused between sentences, the man next to her leaned over and asked her if there was any coffee available. She got up with him and left the conference room. I looked at my watch to note the time.

The meeting continued, though most every question posed came back to the realization that we needed to wait for her return. The wait became so long I almost asked—and I regret that I didn't—to stop the meeting and wait for her. In exactly eight minutes and forty-eight seconds, she returned with the gentleman who was blowing on his steaming cup of coffee. The woman sat back down, *apologized* for her absence, and explained that their coffee maker takes eight-and-a-half minutes to brew.

This was taken as normal. The man with the coffee seemed satisfied. The woman seemed unphased. But the woman—despite being the expert holder of all information we needed—was pulled out of a meeting to serve a man coffee. On top of that, she did it *willingly,* and without questions or visible resentment. That man could have asked any of the other men in the room, or stepped out and asked the receptionist, who was just on the other side of the door. And the woman could have sent him out in search alone, or said she could get it for him after the meeting. But what I saw pointed out how much men still view women as being in service to them. And we women, despite our best efforts, see ourselves that way, too. Between watching women behave differently in the classroom and get treated differently in the boardroom, I was beginning to feel as if our voices could never quite rise above.

But after I heard those words—spoken over a catchy beat—in the car that night after class I was so overcome with nostalgia that when I pulled into my driveway, I sat for a moment in quiet reflection. In this day and age, quiet reflection can only get you so far before you are overcome with the need to do an Internet search on your iPhone.

I searched for the lyrics to "Free to Wear Sunscreen," only to discover one of the first Google hits was an article explaining how the song was mistakenly attributed to Kurt Vonnegut. I was at once horrified and embarrassed to learn that one of my favorite Vonnegut passages wasn't even written by him. I was a teen in the throes of high school drama, and was perhaps a bit self-absorbed. So until that moment in the car with the lyrics of "Free to Wear Sunscreen," I hadn't given much thought to whose words they actually were. And I began to wonder if perhaps the words would mean as much to me if they weren't coming from the brilliant mind of one of the more profound American writers there ever was. As I read more, I realized the piece was written by a woman, Mary Schmich, a Pulitzer Prize–winning journalist for the *Chicago Tribune*.

To say the least, I was intrigued to discover a *woman* wrote this. After all, those words had been spoken by a man in the hit song. And until minutes earlier, I had thought they had been *written* by one, too. But knowing it was a woman behind the words suddenly changed them for me. I read the original article and suddenly saw the speech differently. It wasn't a wise, brilliant satirist sighing and laughing at youth today, telling them to chill the fuck out. It was a woman, roughly the same age I am now, looking around at other women and reminding us to be kind to our bodies and our minds, and, for the love of God, to protect our skin!

This was a revelation. Suddenly the words had new meaning. A woman, a well-known and well-respected columnist, was using her platform at a newspaper to give some pithy advice to other women, and her words were usurped. Her voice was taken, by men.

I've matured enough to realize I wasn't all that wise at fourteen, and there are numerous other people *now* whom I would rank above Kurt Vonnegut. But I was so angry to realize how much Mary Schmich had been silenced, her words taken and therefore changed, by a voice deeper than hers. But somehow, someway, her words made it through all the clutter. After all, there's only one thing I've done every day, consistently, for the past eighteen years: wear sunscreen.

OWN YOUR PATCH OF SOIL

My first job out of college was great, and in retrospect, I learned more than I realized while I was there. I worked in the marketing department for a well-known nonprofit agency that raised more than $25 million annually. My job there was to plan and execute five massive events every year: a 5K run (with thousands of runners), a volleyball tournament (with hundreds of players), a fancy gala (with hundreds of dinner guests), a citywide volunteer day (with thousands of volunteers), and a celebration of accomplishing our fundraising goal (with hundreds of donors). It was a lot of responsibility for a twenty-two-year-old, but I never once stopped to acknowledge that. In fact, I was already aiming for a promotion within the first year. This is where competition and comparison (see Tactic One, and stop it!) rears its ugly head. I believed I was doing far more work—and better work!—than my peers.

During the winter holidays of my first year on the job, the executive director came by my cubicle and told me she was putting me in charge of decorating the entire office. This meant adorning the Christmas tree, hanging garland and twinkly lights, and spraying fake snow in the corners of the office windows. Rest assured, this demand had little, if anything, to do with my gender (most of the staff were female) and everything to do with my age and rank. I can't tell you how pouty I was about this. Didn't she know who I was? I planned events for thousands, dammit! I was the founder and president of the environmental club in college! I read Vonnegut!

Begrudgingly, I accepted the box of decorations and got to work. When I was halfway through hanging the ornaments on the tree, the executive director came out of her office and showed me a better way to do it. This infuriated me. I'm a college graduate! My degree is not in ornamentation! I don't care to be taught this drivel! After seeing her pick on me a few more times about my garland technique, several of my coworkers came out of their offices to help. One put on holiday music loudly in the lobby, and we wound up breaking out eggnog, having a dance party, and enjoying a slow day that chilly November. Many good lessons came out of that tree-decorating. I learned a great deal about working with a team and relying on my peers for guidance and support. I learned not to ever take any kind of fun at work for granted, no matter how menial the task might seem. And, perhaps best of all, I learned how to decorate the crap out of a tree. I had been such a little shit about it in the moment. I thought I was above it, but I wasn't, and I never will be.

In my current job, I'm able to see that those things we think we are above are actually some of the most important work we do. The higher climb doesn't happen without looking below. These are the chances to get dirty, dig down, and sprout up. As the leader of a graduate program, I'm responsible for high-level decisions like curriculum, class scheduling, admissions, and advising. But I also still update the website, order any swag (we have the nicest pens around), and even clean up classrooms that have been left in disarray. I don't feel above any of it. In those small moments, I believe I'm showing my biggest commitment.

But I've noticed that some of my students see their job description as a checklist to accomplish. Once they've checked off the boxes, they are ready to move on to the next challenge and surpass their peers. Jess, for example, was in my office, upset about her current job. "I'm about to have a master's degree, and I'm being asked to do the most menial work," she groaned. When I asked her what she would rather be doing, she said, "I just want a job that is more challenging. I *need* to be challenged." I understood her struggle. We are all looking toward the next level in our climb, sometimes at the expense of more experience, or at the expense of our peers. We all want to be challenged and satisfied in our role. We go in search of greener grass instead of burrowing down in the soil in which we are planted. I'm not suggesting women take bullshit tasks that are assigned to them because women often get stuck with certain tasks (such as cleaning out the office fridge and planning birthday parties). But I am suggesting people understand the difference between truly degrading tasks and tasks we just perceive to be beneath us rather than true opportunities from which to learn.

I asked Jess a tough question: "Are you doing the most you can in the job you have?" She shrugged. "No, but that's only because this is not where I want to be."

"I get that," I said. "But what are you doing within the parameters of the job to make it more challenging for yourself?" She thought for a minute. "Well, there are a few things I think the organization could do to improve the process in my area."

"That's great. What else?"

"There's probably some opportunity to work across departments on some projects."

"Perfect. What else?"

"There's actually a professional conference I want to attend that I think could help me in my job."

"Excellent. Ask your employer to pay for it. What else?" She stopped for a minute and started smiling. "That's a lot right there, isn't it?"

That next level is a great thing to strive for, but it's never the thing on which to focus. Bloom where you are planted. Take where you are, with what you have, and make it something all your own. Accept the box of garland and twinkly lights and go deep. Roles are created not to be permanent structures, but dynamic and changing positions of influence (yes, even those super low-level jobs). And you are not created to be a permanent cog, so be a dynamic influencer where you are *right now*. The next level is coming, but first you must get your footing before you can step up. It's like that summer when I transferred a crepe myrtle from our front yard to the backyard: It survived the transfer and thrived in the new environment because I gave it time to grow where I had planted it.

• • •

I've required group work in nearly every class I've ever taught. This is always met with groans, trepidation, and pleading. Every student hates group work. And yet, instructors around the world continue to assign it.

I understand all the belly aching. I remember my own struggles in group assignments, always convinced I was the one who did all the work. I was always the first to take the lead in a group assignment, helping to dole out roles and offering to be the point person for everyone. I still vividly remember my group member Kendall in an undergrad physics class. Oh, the stories I conjured up about Kendall to justify her unforgivable behavior: She must not be invested in our project because she has too much on her plate. She must not be responding to my emails because she doesn't have Internet access in her dorm room (this was a thing in my day). Or, she must come from a broken home because what kind of sick bitch won't come to our regularly scheduled group meetings?

When I became a professor, I vowed that I would never subject my students to such asinine assignments. But, in the way that becoming a mother has made me see the wisdom of my own parents, I quickly came to see these group assignments serve a worthy purpose. They offer a chance to experience group dynamics, which are the cornerstone of nearly every aspect of our personal and professional lives. They allow for various individual strengths to be harnessed and utilized and for the compensation of individual weaknesses. Further—and this shouldn't be underestimated—group projects take much less time to grade than individual assignments.

Despite all those benefits, the students still protest group work, so much so that, over time, I've changed my group assignments to accommodate the many problems I've faced throughout the years. Now my students have to develop a team contract and are graded on their ability to adhere to it. Also, they can now evaluate their fellow group members at the end of the semester. And, most important, students are graded as individuals, not as a group.

Despite all these fail-safes, every semester I get complaints of group members not pulling their weight, responding to emails, or turning in quality work. Which means there are clearly some people who cannot be motivated, coerced, pressured, or punished into doing good work or trying their hardest. This, perhaps, is the biggest lesson we all must learn.

Recently, three students came in before class started because they urgently needed to speak with me. They were concerned about their group project, which was due in two weeks. They were equal parts angry and worried as they explained how terrible their group member had been and how fearful they were that their grades would be compromised. I sympathized with their agony, and I understood where that pressure came from. For the student, it all comes down to credit. Literally. Students don't want a bad grade. They want credit for their hard work, and they don't want anyone jeopardizing that. And I know students believe that once they graduate, they will never have to be part of a group project again.

But here's the thing: I've never done any job in a vacuum. I've always had to work either within a team or with the help of other departments. When I was responsible for planning large events at the nonprofit agency, I always had a crew of volunteers and other staff members to help me through it. When I was a waitress, I was responsible for taking orders, but not for cooking the food. But in school, students are trained to believe their individual efforts are all that matters. It's an individual grade, a personal transcript, and a single diploma. Much like how animals that have successfully adapted to zoo life have become completely unable to survive the wild, the entire educational ecosystem is designed to focus on the individual, only to then release these individuals into a working world in which everyone must collaborate.

My husband worked for an oil and gas company for many years. This is true for many in Oklahoma, but it was particularly interesting that Jim worked in the energy field because he's a writer. Having moved back from Los Angeles, where he worked on scripts for ABC, Jim found his skill set was desirable in the corporate world, where engineers and petroleum experts needed their work succinctly expressed to the layman. He was part of a seven-person communications team. There was a team leader—his direct supervisor—who reported to one of the top three men in the global company.

Jim has always had a two-prong professional philosophy: 1) work as hard as you can to be as good as you can at what you are assigned to do; and 2) stay above the fray. So in the job, he did exactly that. He worked hard at what he was assigned to do—translate big, complicated processes in the energy industry into easily digestible explanations for customers—and he didn't get bogged down in office gossip or drama. Jim is ambitious, sure, but it always puzzled me that he never worried too much about advancing at work. That's supposed to be the individual goal, right? Work hard to promote yourself and your standing within a company? But he was always more concerned with mastering the individual tasks he was given and being a model team player, assured *that* was the way to move up. After a while it became obvious that not everyone on his team was an equal contributor. Some were always coming to work late or leaving early. Others wouldn't produce to the best of their ability. A few were strong and loyal, always giving their best efforts. But most days, Jim felt like he was doing more than his fair share.

Eventually, the division was restructured and their team leader was reassigned to manage a similar team overseas. This left an opening for the director of the department, and Jim decided he would apply. Not surprisingly, everyone else on the team applied as well. For a few awkward weeks, each team member was called up to a board room to meet with the top executives of the company. Only Jim was called back for a second interview. While in the room, the executives said they were impressed with Jim for two reasons: 1) he had worked hard to master the tasks they'd given him; and 2) he was the only person they interviewed who didn't claim to be the biggest asset to the team—many of the applicants had gone so far as to blame others on the team. Jim smiled slightly and said, "Well, I was hoping my work would speak for itself." He was offered the director position the next day.

Which is not unlike the dynamics I witness every time I assign a group project. Sometimes I dictate which people will be in each group; sometimes I let students self-select. (Trust me, I've tested both strategies and neither guarantees better group dynamics). Given my view of the classroom and my knowledge of each individual student's abilities, I can easily tell where there will be problems. The student who never turns in her individual assignments on time is about to upset the two perfectionists with whom she was just grouped. The student who is always a bit overbearing and controlling is about to ruffle the feathers of the two laid-back guys in her group. The student who is always just a little too sloppy with his edits is about to terrify the two rule-followers on his team.

I've never once had a complaint about a group member that came as a surprise. The students who get complaints from their group members are always the students I've had to speak to about their individual assignments as well. The performance of individual group members is incredibly apparent to the instructor of a class. And, as was obvious in my husband's case, it is apparent to the executives of a corporation as well. Just like stretched-thin, Internet-less Kendall from my own college experience; even though we did well on our group project, she ultimately didn't pass the class.

Good work is noticeable; bad work is, too. Hard work is as apparent as laziness. And credit is never worth seeking; it will come to those who earn it. What those three students didn't realize that morning they came to talk to me was that there's an obvious and constant truth in group work: Those people who struggle in a group setting are usually struggling individually as well. You can't control those with whom you get assigned to work. But you can control your role—and your attitude—within the group. Don't worry unduly about those in your group who don't seem to pull their weight; they always get what is coming to them. And don't worry unduly about rising above and out to the next level. The good work—and who is responsible for it—is always apparent to those assigning the credit.

BE YOUR OWN BIGGEST FAN

When I was in the sixth grade, I competed in the science fair at the regional level. I had done an experiment with card games analyzing the statistical probability of beating a computer versus beating a human dealer. When the two judges came around, they asked just a couple of questions before starting to move on to the sad plant-based project beside me. I put my hands out and stopped them. "That's it?" I asked. They looked at each other and shrugged. "Well, I'm not done," I said, and continued telling them about the validity of my analyses and the application of my results. The more excitedly I talked about my project, the more excited the judges became. I took first place that day and went on to be a state finalist. Don't worry, years later I did manage to find a prom date.

People will often work hard to achieve something, and, once they do, they believe their work is done. But when the goal is met, the work is just beginning. Just because my students had the credentials to get into graduate school doesn't automatically mean they will be successful. They've got to show me what they are made of with every assignment. And once they graduate with the degree, it will be time to promote the credentials they just earned. On the flip side, just because I'm the professor doesn't mean students will automatically engage with my lecture or join in the class discussion. I've got to be engaging, dynamic, and knowledgeable. Same thing at home. Just because I am my kids' mom doesn't mean I will automatically make them macaroni and show them love. (Don't worry, I do both. Constantly.)

As the interviews for the CEO position went on, I began to notice that a lot was riding on what the candidate did when they walked into the room. The candidate we eventually selected was a highly qualified and educated woman. But before we knew the true extent of her qualities, one member on the search committee wrote this down after her introductions: She *owned the room.*

This may sound like terrible news if you feel introverted, shy, or simply incapable of owning a room. But it's actually good news—you can own any room you walk into. The candidate didn't come cartwheeling into the room with a cheer. She simply walked in confidently, shook everyone's hand, smiled, and seemed open. From there, she could sell us on herself because we were primed and ready to hear.

This is called the *halo effect*, a term coined by psychologist Edward Thorndike back in the 1920s. He conducted a study in which he interviewed commanding officers about their subordinate officers' qualities, like leadership, intelligence, and loyalty. Thorndike wanted to see if the commanding officer's perception of one quality of a subordinate would impact their perception of the other qualities of the same subordinate. He discovered that, in fact, it did. Those commanding officers who ranked their subordinate officers high on one trait also rated them high on almost all other traits; the reverse was true with negative traits. Essentially, it means that your overall impression of a person impacts how you view their individual characteristics. If you find someone attractive, you're more likely to think they are smart as well. If you find someone to be warm and approachable, you're inclined to think they are kind and rational. So, if I felt that you "owned the room," I'm more likely to also think you are competent, nice, and ethical. Essentially, you have the power to own the terms. What you lead with casts a glow—positive or negative— over everything else you are.

When it comes to those group presentations I require of my students, I demand a lot of show-selling. In the classes I taught earlier in my career (before I'd developed a reputation passed down by previous classes), students would come to these presentations in shorts, ripped jeans, or once, pajamas. The assumption was: This is school; it's not like it matters how I present myself. But I continually reminded students that they had to take ownership of the terms. You want to be taken seriously? Then *make* me take you seriously. Just because you're up in front of the class with a PowerPoint presentation behind you doesn't mean I have to invest in what you are saying. You want the job? Just because your resume got you an interview doesn't mean you don't have to sell me on your capabilities. Understand that what you put out there is what will be expected of you.

• • •

There are people in this world who claim they love surprises. But the reality is that no one does. Sure, people like unexpected birthday parties and a delivery of flowers at work. But no one ever gasps in excitement over flat tires or IRS audits. I learned this one summer in college when I worked as a waitress at a high-end restaurant on a lake.

I gained a lot of knowledge that summer. I learned how to balance a large tray—filled with steaming hot plates—gracefully on my shoulder. I learned the ideal temperature for preparing each cut of meat. I learned how to open a wine bottle while continuing to talk and charm those at the table (that one still comes in handy). And I learned how to deduce dessert orders from slurring drunk people (also, oddly handy). But the biggest lesson I took away from my three months in the food industry was how to manage expectations.

The restaurant I worked at was a bona fide hot spot. The wait for a table was consistently over an hour. So running out of a certain dish or a particular vintage wasn't uncommon.

In my first few weeks, I would never volunteer that we were out of prime rib or that the case of 1994 Chateau Montelena didn't arrive in time for the weekend. Instead, I'd bet the odds that my patrons wouldn't request either and the issue would never arise. But inevitably, they'd want a hearty steak with a good red wine. And when I would have to quietly inform them we were out of the Porterhouse—after they had their minds made up—they were always frustrated. My tips suffered greatly in those instances.

One night, I saw a veteran waitress approach a table of Saturday night regulars, predictably in their polos and boat shoes. She said "hello" and told them how nice it was to see them all again, and then immediately informed them, with a cute cluck of the tongue, "Just so you are aware, we have run out of lobster tonight."

I expected to see these wealthy men stand up, grab the hands of their impossibly thin wives, and storm out of the restaurant, never to return. But instead, they shrugged and asked the waitress what else she'd recommend. It was the first time I understood that people, even yacht-owning people, can be reasonable and rational in the face of disappointment.

So long as they have a heads-up.

Imagine how much more easily people could handle difficult life transitions if they just knew what exactly to expect. I mean, giving birth and caring for an infant isn't exactly like being told duck l'orange is no longer on the menu, but the idea is the same. Could someone, anyone, have clued me in on what it's like to hear your infant cry for hours on end? Was it too much to ask that someone give me a heads-up about the after care for episiotomies?

I took this idea, one that I learned as a young wait-ress, and I've carried it into most every aspect of my life. I believe my response to Jim's marriage proposal (after the YES!) was something along the lines of, "But just so you are aware, I need to talk out all my feelings. All the time. I get uncomfortable with too much seriousness, and there's a chance I fart in my sleep." So he went into the marriage knowing full well what to expect.

In parenting, I try to let my kids know what's happen-ing. I tell them in the morning what their day holds. And while I hope a few exciting and unpredictable adventures await, they seem to take comfort in knowing that Daddy will take them to school, Mommy will pick them up, and we are having chicken for dinner.

And I try, as best I can, to use this technique at work because, in my role, managing expectations is paramount. I've got to present myself and my classes in a way that makes the expectations for class and the graduate program clear. If I'm a person who's always responsive, professional, and hardworking, that will be the expectation of those who learn under me.

One area where I work the hardest to clearly define expectations is the syllabus for each course. It's also the hardest area for me because I have about three pages to manage everyone's expectations of how the next four months of their life will go. And, you know, get them excited to spend that much time with me.

For whatever reason, I always forget how deeply students care about the syllabus. But every semester, when my syllabi get posted a week before class starts, I'm reminded of how much people hate surprises and how far they will go to avoid them. Last semester, mere minutes after posting a syllabus for each of my classes, I had a river of emails flood my inbox. These emails are never fun to open because never once has a student emailed just to say, "Wow, that's a damn fine syllabus! Garamond? You dawg!"

Instead, emails come in with questions about the schedule. Did I really mean to put those two due dates on back-to-back weeks? Or questions about the textbook. Can I just use an older edition my best friend's boyfriend has? There are questions about my office hours. Do I ever meet at 7:00 a.m.? And even questions about my attention to detail. Did I mean to have that typo?

I get it. When I was a college student I couldn't wait for the syllabus. I wanted to be fully aware of what I could expect and what would be expected of me. I had a need to put all the due dates in my planner and to try to gauge the personality of the professor by the tone of the text.

That's a lot of pressure riding on one document. It not only has to excite students, it also has to assure them. Because no one likes surprises.

Least of all the wealthy restaurant patrons in search of top-shelf vodka. Or newlyweds braving the adventures of cohabitation. New mothers overwhelmed by their responsibility. Children feeling scared by all the unknowns of life. Students fearing a tough semester.

And yet.

One night at the restaurant a customer was upset because our menu had changed and his favorite dish had disappeared. To compensate for the foul mood this put him in, I surprised him with a free dessert. The size of my tip that night was certainly unexpected. In our first year of marriage, Jim had to have emergency surgery. He was pleasantly surprised to discover what an excellent caretaker I can be. And one day, when I dropped Lowery off at school, I promised her Jim would be picking her up. She said it again to confirm. I promised. But my mother unexpectedly came into town that afternoon and asked to pick her up from school. The look on my child's surprised face, according to my mother, was the stuff dreams are made of.

Some of the most meaningful evaluations I have ever received were in courses in which the students' expectations for the class were extremely low. One wrote that he didn't think the topic would be interesting, and another commented that she had never heard anything about the professor. Yet many seemed pleasantly surprised at how much they liked the class.

Which leaves me wondering if maybe people do like surprises. I mean, I get it when expectant mothers want to wait to see the gender of their baby at birth. But even they know what species to expect. Or maybe it's just that people like to be surprised when they know the limited, and possible, outcomes. Then again, our children love to get surprises no matter what it is. I can guarantee that a surprise trip to Disney World would elicit the same response as the toy in a Cheerios box, so maybe people just like the *idea* of surprises.

Or maybe it's not knowing the possible outcomes or liking the potential of surprises; maybe it's that people are adaptable. A friend of mine became unexpectedly pregnant, despite vowing she was done birthing babies. And yet, she claims that baby is the greatest surprise she's ever received. So maybe the unexpected that might catch people off guard, throw them off their game, and disrupt their routine is something they adapt to and grow to appreciate. Maybe people like surprises in retrospect.

So where's the balance between setting expectations and enjoying the surprises of life? How do I set the expectations for my marriage, kids, and students? Should I let my husband deal with unexpected changes in my personality, mood, and life goals? Should I expect them in his? Should I control my children's environment as best I can to help them feel as secure as possible? Or do I just teach them how to deal with the unknown? And should I work even harder to constantly clarify the expectations of education? Or should I just encourage my students to enjoy the ride? I'm desperate for a solid and definitive answer. But that's to be expected.

OWN THE FAIL

Taking ownership of the terms also means taking ownership of the failures along the way. You see, few, if any, of us get it right the first time. My colorist would agree. People get it wrong sometimes. Or, they simply change their minds. Seventy percent of college students change their major at least once; most will change their major three times before they graduate. And this is a great thing. Why? Because each wrong gets you closer to what's right.

Haralick and Elliott, two researchers in the field of computer engineering, gave us a term for this idea: the *fail-first principle*. As engineers for artificial intelligence, their principle is a mathematical probability—not about choosing a major in college—but the basic premise is applicable anywhere. Basically, they posit that if you first test the solution you believe is most likely to fail, then you'd be more likely to know which is the correct solution; in other words, employ a process of elimination. Once they could fail one test, they could more confidently go forth with the next.

All too often, people are terrified to fail. But even the construct of failure is arbitrary, and it's usually driven by what we think others perceive. Let's say you try out a new career, but you end up not liking it and deem the attempt a failure. Well, calling it a failure is on you. Owning the terms suggests you look at that as a fail-first, and now you're closer to where you want to be in your career. Let's say you try something and it is deemed—by anyone's account—as a failure, like getting fired. Though it's tough to overcome a swift life transition like that, it can still be considered a step closer to the right answer. While most of my students are determined to be, and ultimately are, successful in graduate school, that isn't the case for everyone. In fact, I've had a few students who fail the program. One such student came to see me before parting ways with the university. She marched into my office yelling; I hadn't helped her enough, the program's standards were out of whack, and her career was now ruined. Her anger was so raw that I didn't know how exactly to respond. So I just told her this wasn't the end of anything, but the beginning of something she didn't know yet (and I know at the time that must have seemed condescending and possibly hurtful). But a year later, she called to say she realized she had been trying to force something—the graduate degree—when it never was the right fit. She said she was now in a job she loved—in which she felt valued and respected—and wouldn't have gotten there if she hadn't officially failed out of grad school. Her anger in my office that day was what anger always is: the outward manifestation of fear. While I couldn't predict where she would end up, I also never doubted she'd be okay. With her, as with so many others, the quickest path to success was through failure.

The point is, you get a lot of chances for a do-over. Seemingly endless chances. This doesn't mean you can't mess up so royally with something, such as a boss, a degree, or a spouse. You may not get a second chance there. But you get them elsewhere. When you think about failure, think also about success—they are two sides of the same coin. Failure is nothing to be afraid of; it is the moment where you can step in and refuse to accept anything but another chance to get it right.

• • •

Despite being the more grounded of the two of us, my husband is quite the optimist—when he's not being a realist or a pessimist. When we first started dating, Jim planned a romantic evening out for us. This included seeing the new exhibition at a museum, drinks at my favorite bar, and dinner at a restaurant I had promised myself I'd never patronize again. While Jim's default is to always let me have my way, that night he refused. He drove us to the restaurant with me protesting the entire way. When we pulled into the lot, he put the car in park, shut off the engine, turned to me, and said, "I'm about to give you an overlay experience."

I blushed at his forwardness, but he then explained what he meant by "overlay." He believed that all bad experiences can be redone, with the hopes of having a better experience the second time. So by taking me to a restaurant in which I'd had a bad experience, he was determined to overlay it with a good one. And it worked.

We had such a fantastic date that night, the restaurant is now one of our favorite spots. While this instance seemed small, Jim's overlay idea became a substantial component of our relationship. We have reexperienced numerous restaurants, various trips, and dozens of movies together. But it also became somewhat of a philosophy of our life together: No bad experience is the final word.

Sometimes the overlays were small: Jim rewatching *Annie Hall* with me and finally agreeing it had merit (he's still bitter it beat out *Star Wars* for best picture). And sometimes they were significant: the birth of our second child overlaying the experience of our first. The experience birthing our first child was a bad one. It involved an incredibly long labor, hours of pushing, extreme tearing (men, your life is a cakewalk), excruciating PUPPS rash *after* delivery (Google Image this, but not before dinner), no milk supply leading to my daughter's severe dehydration and readmission into the hospital, the horror of trying to defecate after a vaginal delivery (seriously, as a gender we need to talk about this more), and postpartum depression. It ran the gamut of horrible experiences.

But on the eve of our second daughter's birth, my husband assured me the experience would overlay the first. He even argued the more horrible the first experience, the greater the overlay. And dammit if he wasn't right again. I hardly even noticed I'd delivered London. It was a short labor with only a handful of pushes, no tearing, no rash, no dehydration issues, and I didn't bat an eye taking a shit after birth. I even escaped postpartum depression. I came home with a quiet, sweet, sleepy baby who politely existed in our lives the first few weeks as if she didn't want to bother anyone. This made me believe I was ready to take on one of life's greatest challenges: the family vacation.

Because Memorial Day was upon us, we decided that an overnight stay somewhere close would be the perfect way to spend our first vacation as a family of four. We chose a town that was a two-hour drive from home. I found the perfect hotel that boasted a beautiful pool and its walking distance to family-friendly restaurants. I bought tickets to a science museum and the zoo, and I made sure the botanical gardens were open over the holiday break.

The night before we left, I packed more brilliantly than I'd ever packed before. I had a bag of snacks that were neither choking hazards nor produced crumbs. I had all the baby's gear: portable crib, stack of diapers, wad of burp cloths, onesies, blankets, swaddle sacks, and lotion. I had all the toddler gear: books, dolls, underwear, clothes, eight pairs of shoes, a sun hat, and detangler. I had swimsuits for all four of us, sunscreen, the double stroller, and chargers for all electronic devices. I even had the fucking *Frozen* soundtrack.

The morning we were set to depart, Jim and I stopped for coffee and gas and were thrilled with ourselves for getting on the road at the exact time for which we had aimed and synchronized our watches. During the drive, the uninterrupted conversation and peacefully sleeping children lured us both into a false sense of security.

We had a pleasant time when we stopped for lunch. And the first destination—the science museum—was a huge success. But before dinner, with everyone waiting in the hotel room while I fed the baby, things started to unravel. It began with a slight burning in my right eye. I felt no relief when I took my contacts out and put them on the nightstand. My husband joked that I had pink eye. I laughed, until I looked over at Lowery and noticed her left eye was gunky. And pink. Luckily, my brilliant packing included every single medication in our bathroom, even a half empty bottle of antibiotic eye drops. I'm not implying that trying to get eye drops into an uncooperative preschooler ruined the trip. But it sure worked up a nice sweat before dinner.

Once the baby was fed and all infected eyes were treated, we decided to walk to a nearby restaurant. I had London strapped to my chest, and Lowery held my husband's hand as we strolled out of the hotel to discover it was sprinkling. Slightly. As we walked, however, the slight sprinkle turned into a light rain. One block down, and the light rain became an average rain, in which puddles start to form. Another half a block down and the rain started to pick up to the point where my husband hoisted our child to his hip, ineffectively put his hand on top of her head to block the water, and started to run. Because I had an infant strapped to the front of me and was wearing sandals with no tread, I slowed down and clutched the brick walls of the buildings we were passing. By the time we got to the restaurant door, rain was falling in a manner normally associated with hurricanes or movies about shipwrecks. I'm not implying that getting drenched with rainwater on our walk to the restaurant ruined our trip. But it sure cooled us off from all the eye-drop wrestling.

Once safely inside the restaurant, we were told there would be a thirty-minute wait for a table. This didn't worry me. In my brilliant packing I had managed to bring a small backpack filled with coloring books and stickers to occupy my three-year-old in such a situation. But after we had been waiting an hour, all the stickers were placed and all the pages were colored. When our name was finally called, we were taken back to a table surrounded by roughly fifteen other empty tables. In fact, the restaurant was nearly vacant. I'm not implying that waiting more than an hour for a table when there were clearly no other people occupying it ruined our trip. But it certainly allowed us time to work up an appetite.

Another hour passed before our meal was delivered. The waiter explained that the delay was because the restaurant was "slammed." The only bright spot of the three-hour meal was a balloon artist who came to our table as we were trying to pay the bill. Lowery asked for a bunny rabbit, which he quickly made to her extreme enjoyment. She was so excited, in fact, that she leapt out of her seat to come show me her new animal, tripped over the balloon artist's foot and collided with the concrete floor. She screamed a scream not normally possible from such small lungs. This awoke our infant, who promptly tried to rival her sister's volume. I scooped up my three-year-old and headed to the lobby with both children screaming uncontrollably. With no option, I sat down on the floor to feed the baby while using my one free arm to wipe the blood off my other child's knees, all while my husband chased down our waiter so he could pay the bill. The screaming from both children lasted the entire walk back to the hotel. I'm not implying that the awful restaurant experience ruined our trip. But I do think it was responsible for putting all four of us in a foul mood.

Back in our hotel room and in dry clothes, Lowery was beginning to exhibit signs of mental instability. She pulled everything out of every bag and all the pillows off the bed and then ran to the bathroom and attempted to lock herself in. I tried to help my husband with her antics, but I was occupied by our inconsolable infant.

For over an hour I worked to calm my inexplicably crying baby, while my husband resorted to every disciplinary tactic ever invented to try to calm down her wound-up sister. Lowery is strong-willed and independent; to that we are accustomed. But this night was like nothing we'd ever seen. She had gone full-on Linda Blair.

Meanwhile, our infant, who had barely uttered a peep in her first few weeks of life, was screaming as though she'd just realized she had exited the womb. At one point, the front desk called to raise concerns about the noise level. We could barely hear each other over the two screaming girls.

"I don't negotiate with terrorists!" my husband yelled at one point as our three-year-old attempted to stick her head through a coat hanger.

"When is your vasectomy scheduled?!" I hollered over the high-pitched screech of our infant.

Lowery, who by that point had opened the two complimentary bottles of water and poured them in the toilet, fought our demands that she get on the bed and go to sleep. She cried and screamed and pouted and, to my complete horror, spit.

Watching my child—my sweet, typically well-behaved child—literally spit at us made something inside me snap. I yelled. I yelled louder than the screaming children. Louder than I'd ever yelled. And when I stopped, Lowery looked at me, completely unfazed by my outburst, and yelled back, "I'm just *not* tired!"

With that pronouncement, she threw herself dramatically on the bed. As her head hit the pillow, even before the rest of her body had landed, she was completely asleep. My husband and I looked at each other in shock, not even registering that London had miraculously stopped crying as well and had passed out asleep in my arms. Jim tiptoed over to Lowery's bed and covered her with a blanket. I laid the baby gently down in the crib and we silently crawled into bed together, trembling while we held each other like Leo and Kate in the icy waters. I'm not implying that our three-year-old ruined our family vacation, but she totally did.

The next morning, Lowery popped up looking refreshed and happy. She bounced over to our bed to give us kisses. We rose up like two hungover frat boys to kiss her back. We had taken the zoo trip away from her the night before as a failed attempt to negotiate, which left us with only one remaining activity. The activity that had most excited Lowery. The activity that was making her jump up and down on the bed, gleefully laughing. I handed her swimsuit to her and called down to the front desk to check the pool hours. It was only 6:00 a.m.

"Oh, I'm sorry to tell you this," said the desk clerk. "The pool is currently closed."

"I figured it was too early," I replied. "What time will it open?"

"You've misunderstood me. It's *closed*. For repairs."

To avoid another meltdown, we promised Lowery we would let her play in the sprinkler when we got back home. This pacified her, and she happily helped us pack. But when we got in the car, Jim and I both cursed under our breath to see the rain clouds ahead.

Ten minutes into our journey home, a mere eighteen hours after the trip began, Lowery said she needed to use the bathroom. The last sign we passed said the next rest stop was thirty miles ahead. Lowery began to cry, yelling that she really needed to go and couldn't hold it.

Jim and I contemplated our options, which were a) to stuff all of London's diapers down Lowery's pants while going eighty miles per hour down the highway, or b) to pull off on the side of the road. Neither seemed advisable, so instead we sped, promising Lowery candy if she could hold it. (I wasn't going up for mother of the year this trip.)

When we made it to the rest stop, Lowery bounced out of the car and ran next to me holding her crotch. She perched herself on the toilet, but I heard nothing. Pure silence.

"I don't have to go any more," she smiled up at me.

Rather than leave her there on the toilet, get back in the car, and drive away, I'll always praise myself for deciding to take her with us.

Back in the car and ten more minutes down the road, London began screaming. Loudly. We contemplated our options: a) me crawling in the back seat while the car went ninety down the highway, or b) pulling off to the side of the road. Neither was advisable, so we drove another twenty solid minutes with our infant screaming like a tornado siren.

When we finally stopped, I jumped in the back seat, and the moment I placed the pacifier in her mouth, before her lips could even seal around it, she fell asleep. Back on the road again, Lowery softly said, "Okay, I really do have to go this time."

After what seemed like an eternity, we pulled into our driveway. We sat there with the engine running and rain beating down on the hood. Both children were finally sleeping. After a few moments of silence, tears began rolling down my cheeks. When my gentle crying became audible sobbing, Jim turned to look at me. At first his face was twisted with concern, but then it morphed into an enormous grin.

"Why are you smiling?" I said, as snot started collecting on my upper lip.

"Because," he said with a laugh, "just imagine the overlay."

• • •

The bottom line is: Own it. Own who you are, own what you want, own when you fail, and own the overlay back to success. Take control over how you tell the story of your life. Speak up and out about yourself; let your voice be heard. When I think about how many of those candidates we interviewed for the CEO position, I struggle to remember all the particular lines on resumes or all the various answers to the many questions we posed. But I clearly remember one candidate who—while nearly perfect on paper—came in and sat down and waited to talk until she was spoken to. When we asked her to tell us a little about herself, she said, "What do you want to know?" It was a small moment, one that was easily brushed past, but it was a moment she lost out on owning the narrative—leading with her voice and crafting her story. She was waiting on us to set the terms. She didn't get eliminated because of that one line, of course. But the candidate whom we selected? Well, remember, she came in and owned the room.

The Closer
for TACTIC THREE

- **Control** the terms. Call the shots for yourself. Own up to your role in your success and failure.

- **Communicate** those terms. If you carry yourself like a winner, you become a winner. Tell yourself constantly that you're a winner. Tell others you are, but, you know, perhaps more sparingly.

- **Challenge** yourself! Whatever it is you're doing right now can be done even better, or differently. Don't wait around for others to hand you challenges and promotions. Create them where you are.

- **Champion** yourself! Show 'em what you're made of. Not too much, or we'll all start to hate you a little. But give people a reason to buy whatever it is you're selling.

- **Change** your mindset around failure. You're not going to ruin your life or screw up your future if you fail. In fact, you're going to improve your life and your future when you do. Failure is the seed; success is the bloom.

GIVING

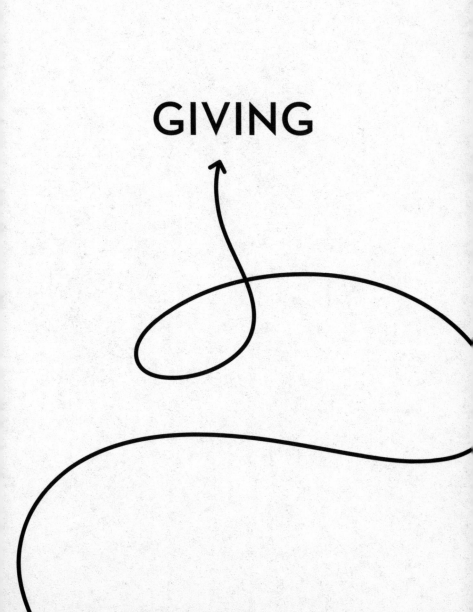

TACTIC FOUR
Never Give Your All

Do you know what single message women are exposed to more than any other? It's this: *Don't put your feminine products in the toilet.* But a close second has to be this: *You can't have it all.* We are told this in a variety of ways—that we can't expect to make it all work. You can't juggle the career and the baby; can't be happily married and travel the globe for your job; can't put too much strain on the internal plumbing system with your tampons. We are told in a lot of ways what we *can't* do, *can't* have, *can't* flush. Oddly enough, getting is related to giving. If we want to get something, we gotta give something. Perhaps our problem is that we don't appreciate that giving and getting can be inversely related; you can sometimes get a little more when you give a little less.

My daughter will often ask for something, maybe a new toy. And if, in a moment of weakness or exhaustion, we agree, she'll immediately say, "Well how about *two* new toys?" She never stops to think about how she'll be able to play with two toys at the same time. She's only worried about the things she wants. Her strategy is stockpiling, staking claim to everything she wants now, what she might want later, and some more stuff for good measure. Women should adopt this mentality, especially because the world is always asking whether it's possible for women to have it all. Our gender, by the way, should never feel compelled to dignify that with a response. But I appreciate that my female students struggle with their ability to *give their all* to everything they want in life.

This isn't just a question I get from current students. I've had countless prospective students come talk to me about graduate school. One young woman came to talk with me about the program, and I've never seen anyone as fired up for graduate school as she was. She expressed her intense desire for the program and conveyed her true passion for the field. As we were wrapping up our meeting, I told her I looked forward to receiving her application. Her hands went up in protest and her face twisted with tension. "Oh, I'm not going to apply right *now*," she said. "I want to wait until it's the right time. You know, so I can really give it my all."

Maybe that was just a turn of phrase, but it's become the rhetoric, and the practice, of my generation of women—this idea of giving your all. Give your children your all. Give your all to your spouse. Give that career of yours all you've got. But all that giving can often make women hesitate in going after something they really want to do.

Look, it's fine if you don't want kids. Okay if you don't want to go to graduate school. And fine if you don't even care all that much about establishing and nurturing a career path. But let's say you do want any or all of those things. If so, then the worst thing you can do is wait around for a time in which you can give it your all.

I won't go into the graphic details of this, but my husband and I planned to get me pregnant while I was in the middle of my doctoral program. We were successful—again, none of your business—but at the time, people thought we were crazy. And sure, it was difficult slogging away at a dissertation with a screaming baby on my lap, but I relished the fact that I was making progress on everything I wanted in this life. I wasn't letting my desire for children interrupt my desire to finish school. Nor was I letting my career put my personal life on hold. Look, sometimes my kid got drive-thru nuggets when I had to run data, and sometimes my dissertation sat idle for weeks while my child was sick. But it was never about being able to give my all to either. If I waited until I had the ability to give my all, I currently wouldn't have a PhD or any children.

We have to stop using phrases like *giving our all,* and we have to stop thinking like this. You physically can't, and emotionally shouldn't, give your *all* to any one thing. So instead, give your *some* to a lot of things. And that's what I want my female students to know. Yes, you can have it all. But not if you put any one aspect of your life on hold to benefit another. Try my daughter's strategy and stockpile everything you want. You can sort it out later. Don't worry about giving your all to each thing at the same time; that's never actually required. Take the pressure off yourself and go have it all by never giving your all.

GIVE A LITTLE OVER A LOT

I often hear people use phrases like, "It's better to do one thing extremely well than a bunch of things just okay." This, I believe, is horseshit. For one thing, it implies that you can only get good at something if it's the only thing you do. So, what's that *one* thing gonna be? Further, it implies that stuff you do over here doesn't also improve your ability on the stuff you are doing over there. We all know football players sometimes study ballet.

I think you should do a bunch of things. All the things. All at the same time. I'm not talking about texting while driving; I'm talking bigger picture here. Multitasking is different than multi-accomplishing. As you go after more goals, you will become increasingly better at all of them, and your skills and knowledge in one area will help inform your skills and knowledge in all the areas. Over time, you will find that if you put a little bit of yourself into a lot of things, you'll end up with more than you ever imagined.

My grandfather was a master at giving a little of himself to a lot of things. He worked as a car mechanic in the army. Later, at nearly thirty years of age, he realized he wanted more than a blue-collar life could offer. He went to college and secured an apartment on campus for his family by serving as the building superintendent. From there, he worked his way through to a PhD in business and finance. Then he climbed up the ladder, eventually retiring as a university vice president. While I knew about his life in academia, I mostly remember him always wearing a gray mechanic's jumper. You see, on the side he also owned an auto repair shop where he restored more than fifty classic cars as a hobby—a passion for cars still deep within him. When my grandparents moved to Oklahoma from Mississippi, he had a wild idea to buy the worst house near the campus, use his know-how to fix it up, and rent it out to students. From there—using his business and finance knowledge from college—he bought another, then another to build up a thriving business on the side. Looking back, it's funny to think that being a vice president at a top university was the least lucrative part of his career.

He achieved that because he didn't invest himself into just one thing, profession, or skill. He gave a little to a lot of things over time. He took nearly fifteen years to complete all his various degree programs, which he did while helping to raise five daughters and working as a mechanic and the on-site property handyman. His side hustles weren't his life's greatest work, but in the case of his rental property business, it *was* the single venture that set up his and my grandmother's retirement. Near the end of his life, I asked him how he did all those things in his career and his response—through slow, deliberate breath—was, "Just try a lot of things. Something is bound to work out." And with a wry smile he added, "Just prepare yourself in case they *all* do."

Women seem to hold themselves back from just doing all the things. And most of our excuses are self-imposed, imaginary, or simply the manifestation of fear. If you are holding yourself back from doing something merely because you don't think you can do two things at once, I'd like to give you a little nudge. In my case, there are days I'm so tired I can barely speak and so overwhelmed I want to crawl into a hole for a few hours. But in truth, those days are rare. Most days are just sort of busy. But they are busy with all the things I love—my kids, my husband, my students, my writing, my volunteer work. The point is, don't compartmentalize your life into sections. Give a little of yourself to a lot of things, and then practice patience. Soon enough you'll turn around and be surprised at how much you have.

• • •

Despite claiming he is never one to give advice, my father has given me plenty of it.

He just hides it well within everyday conversation. When I was younger, I would often accompany my father—a large-animal veterinarian in rural Oklahoma—out on call to deliver a calf or perform surgery on a pig. My relationship with him seemed to transpire mostly at high speeds in a beat-up truck littered with gauze and antiseptic. While in his pickup, bounding over graveled country roads, we had ample time to talk. I'd fill him in on high school drama and he would lightly press me about issues I was refusing to address, like where I wanted to go to college or what I wanted to be when I grew up.

One afternoon, as we loaded the truck, he said he had a riddle for me: Why is there always a pond next to an overpass? I wasn't sure how to respond because I wasn't sure there *was* a pond next to every overpass. But as we drove and I chatted endlessly about my need for guitar lessons, I noticed that every overpass we drove under had a pond within a short distance.

Intrigued, I wrestled with this puzzle for weeks. Was it to help with runoff after heavy rains? Something about fishing permits? Was the turnpike authority in on this? Then one day, my head resting on the window of the passenger side of my dad's truck while we headed to suture a mare's leg, the answer came flooding into my brain.

"The dirt!" I sputtered. "To build an overpass you need dirt!" My father had waited patiently for me to come to the answer on my own. Moments like those are what I thought parenting was all about.

And yet, by and large, I find parenting rarely to be about imparting profound wisdom to my children through intricate puzzles that encourage them to seek their own answers. Instead, I find parenting to be a lot of cooking, cleaning, and dreading the weekends.

My children are young. While I enjoy and treasure my time with them, I sometimes find the weekends to be anxiety-inducing blocks of time. Maybe a part of it is that what we do on the weekends isn't the parenting I was imagining before we had kids. I'm never calmly driving down a dirt road in the pastoral countryside, wind blowing through my hair while giving my daughters a riddle to solve that will profoundly alter their view of the world. And maybe part of it is that my two children are in different life phases, which require very different types of attention, hygiene, and sizes of cantaloupe chunks.

I'm mostly in the kitchen doling out graham crackers and sippy cups. I'm doctoring a largely invisible gash on my oldest's knee, who screams as if the whole leg has been amputated. I'm holding my youngest because, in general, she thinks we should never be apart. I'm misplacing my coffee cup because I keep setting it on shelves up high to avoid it being tipped over by their running through the house. I'm picking up trails of Legos and discarded clothes, helping my youngest potty-train, and hitting Play on *Frozen*. And I'm desperately searching for something we can go do that will occupy—and *satisfy*—both of my kids simultaneously without driving either me or my husband insane.

Every struggle of the weekend seems so insignificant, so simple, so mundane. And explaining why it's so hard to coworkers on Monday is like explaining a dream: so clear and profound in experience, but hazy and insubstantial in expression.

One particular weekend was typical. It was almost identical to the several weekends before it. Yet it was another weekend I wanted to pass over for the next.

It started with our refrigerator. A few weeks earlier we had noticed water seeping from the front of it. When we opened the freezer drawer, we found the bottom covered in a thin sheet of ice. When the repairman came to look at it, he said the problem was that our refrigerator was tilted slightly forward, making it difficult for water to drain out the back normally. He twisted the feet of the refrigerator to level it (this is what you pay the big bucks for) and told us we would need to defrost the freezer. So I spent Friday afternoon clearing out the appliance and sorting everything into piles of "save," "toss," and "what did this start out as?" I kept all the essentials in a cooler filled with ice, bleached the entire refrigerator, and made sure it was bone dry before plugging it back in and restocking. But on Saturday morning, we awoke to find, yet again, a layer of ice in the bottom of the freezer—and a puddle of water on the kitchen floor.

Another repairman came to tell us the first repairman was wrong and that the problem stemmed from one tiny plug on the back of the appliance not being completely connected to another tiny plug. As we watched him gently connect the two tiny hoses together, using nothing but his fingertips—the skilled labor for which we were paying Saturday rates—we began to see the weekend unraveling.

Because I had discarded so much food in the throes of frozen passion, we needed to go to the grocery store. The moment the sliding doors opened into the cool store, London began to scream because she felt cold. Lowery decided she wanted her own cart with which to push around her prized stuffed unicorn. So, with London screaming and Lowery bumping an empty cart with a mythic passenger into every aisle display, we made our way slowly around the store.

While Jim stood in the very deep line to check out, I took the girls for a walk around the frozen food aisle. London, still sobbing, shuffled across the tile floor while Lowery ran up to strangers to ask them why they were buying that kind of mustard or why they needed a cane.

Eventually, we made it out, but as we passed back through the sliding doors, Lowery stopped suddenly, looking stunned and concerned. "My unicorn!" she yelled. And back in we all went to find the missing, mythical beast.

Back at home, the now-repaired refrigerator fully stocked and lunch consumed, we all gathered in the family room for some downtime. Or so I had hoped. You see, the girls can only play for so long before they get a bit too wound up and end up falling over, resulting in traumatic tears. Jim will rush to the side of whomever he is closer to, and I will do the same. We remind them both that they must watch their surroundings and try to avoid collision. When we are sure they understand, we release them from our embrace. They will look at each other, squeal with delight, stand up, and run toward each other, knocking skulls, and the process will repeat itself over and over again. This makes it impossible to ever finish a game of Candy Land and makes me constantly regret choosing tile flooring.

Later, we decided a trip to the library would be a nice way to spend the afternoon, or at least, kill time before bed. From the first mention of going to the library to backing our vehicle out of the driveway, there were forty-five solid minutes of diaper changes, potty breaks, bag packing, snack-eating, sock-finding, and stuffed-animal-selecting chaos. And before Jim could put the car in drive, both kids were sound asleep.

The fifteen-minute drive to the library was the only calm and relaxing respite Jim and I would experience that weekend. We talked quickly and quietly about what all needed to be done before Monday: laundry, dishes, change the lightbulb in the downstairs bathroom, find the vaccination record for Lowery's school enrollment packet, pick up the dry cleaning, and mail the gas bill. Inside the children's section of the library, our kids' faces imprinted with the patterns of their car seats, they seemed delighted to be among all the books and blocks and children.

Lowery tucked her unicorn protectively under her arm and walked boldly up to another young girl reading *Madeline*. As they engaged in what looked like beautiful and magical child's play, London marched over to the building blocks. As I pulled blocks from her mouth and tried to wipe off her tongue through angry screams, I heard yelling and crying among the shelves. Jim sprinted over to find Lowery and the other young girl engaged in a tug of war over Lowery's horned horse. As the other child explained to me that my daughter's inability to share was rude, I looked over to see London trying to stuff blocks down the front of her pants. I rushed over to find her underwear full of more than just blocks.

Jim and I have big plans for our family. We dream about the vacations we want to take with our girls, the conversations we want to have with them, and the morals and values we want to instill. But every weekend, those dreams, ideals, and plans seem just beyond the horizon, across a busy highway with no overpass. But we know it's out there, just beyond the point where we are now, which is, essentially, deep in the ditch. It seems like our minds are constantly reeling with stress over our children, keeping up with the household chores, or fighting for time on the weekends to rest or catch up on work emails. Everything is coming at us at the same time and we aren't sure if all of our small, consistent efforts into so many areas are amounting to anything other than survival.

But this moment in our lives is about the investment and planning, and I'm optimistic that one day soon, maybe even sooner than I think, I'll be able to give my girls riddles to solve on their own, riddles surrounding a beautiful metaphor about life. But not today. Today I have to remember the advice my father gave me when I was younger—advice that he carefully wrapped in a riddle: Why are there ponds next to overpasses?

Because you have to dig down to build up.

DON'T GIVE YOUR CRITICS TOO MUCH ATTENTION

Tess was in my office, upset. She had just taken a new job and was already battling criticism. Her new position was a coveted role at a highly sought-after organization. All eyes, she felt, were on her. Though she was beyond capable of doing the job, she had heard rumors of people saying she wasn't at all qualified. As her eyes became glossy with tears, she confessed she was worried everyone was right. This happens when anyone—*especially* a woman—rises up. With more visibility, and more substantial contribution to anything, comes one absolute guarantee: more chances to be criticized.

The most frightening things in life are always those that are unavoidable, and criticism is no exception. At a certain point, I realized that criticism was coming at me whether I liked it or not. While I still find criticism hard to digest sometimes, I've come a long way in learning how to process it. Every time a student comes to me worried about criticism, I try to push these five points:

1. *Criticism is not created equally.* I'm always fascinated by customer reviews, especially on women's clothing. It seems as if some women write a review just so they can humble-brag about their shape: "I'm 5'3" and weigh 110—mostly breast weight—and the XS was swimming on me!" I'm also intrigued by the wide range of reviews on books. One of the best lessons on criticism and perspective is to look up your absolute favorite book on Goodreads and read (perhaps in horror) what others think of it. The point is that each reader gets an equal chance to post a book review. Each top-heavy woman gets an equal chance to criticize the spring line. But we don't have to accept critiques equally. If you look more closely at the naysayers of any product, book, or sweater vest, you can see that sometimes the reviewer seems either inordinately hard to please or is not the intended audience. Criticisms that seem more measured and come from rational people who *were* the intended audience should get more weight.

Sure, everyone gets an equal voice when it comes to criticism, but you must never give all criticism equal weight. Always consider the source. Those consumers invested in your product are typically not the ones who spew venom. And remember that usually for every one-star review, there's someone out there giving you a high five.

2. *Just because someone says it doesn't make it true.* I received a student evaluation that said, "This professor WILL NOT respond to emails. So don't expect any of her attention." When I read this, I was baffled. The part of my job I know I am the best at is being responsive and attentive. I aim to respond to every email the same day I receive it. I meet with students after class, sometimes for hours. I set up appointments to meet with students, even during winter and summer breaks. Hell, I give students my cell number! Now, maybe there was a student whose email went unanswered, but dear god, *email me again*. Call my cell. Stop by my office. Have my kidney! The point is: I was being criticized for the very thing I prioritize the most. And when I thought about it, I couldn't think of a way I could be any more accessible (perhaps I should be far less) and so I realized that just because someone says it doesn't make it true.

3. *Pan for gold among the rubble.* About three years into my career I started hearing some negative feedback about how I carried myself around campus. A fellow faculty member stopped by and said, "Just so you are aware, some people are saying you are kind of a self-promoter." This is

funny to hear as an academic because my first response was, "Yeah, who isn't?" But then another person, a staff member, told me the same thing. No one would tell me who was saying this, why they were saying it, or what exactly they wanted me to do about it. *How* was I promoting myself? I couldn't get to the bottom, or the source, of this criticism and I felt wholly on the defense. I was out to lunch with a friend, moaning about these criticisms I kept hearing, and he said, "Well, even if this criticism is unfounded, can you find a kernel of truth in there?" When I stopped and thought about it, without focusing on my own hurt feelings, I could see there was. Admittedly, I'm an enthusiastic and expressive person (perhaps not the most common personality traits among academics). And I realized I tend to excitedly talk a lot about my students; jobs they got, research they did, insights they shared in class. While I didn't feel I was shamelessly *self*-promoting, I began to see how my constant enthusiasm for my role could be interpreted as tooting my own horn. This doesn't mean I toned down my enthusiasm—in fact, some of this felt like the regular shit women hear about themselves when they have any kind of success—but it did make me more mindful about certain ways I express it. Criticism is going to be 80 to 90 percent rubble, but shake the pan a little and see if there's any gold. Then throw out everything that is just the stuff of fools.

4. It hurts, but it won't kill you. I once wrote an article for a major print publication. When it went up online I was thrilled to see a handful of nice comments pop up. But then came one that shook me a bit. Then another. And another. I'd never seen such anger spewed over an article that I didn't think was all that controversial. These comments attacked my writing, my teaching, and even my mental stability. While I knew that just because the comments were written didn't make them true—and I was certainly considering the sources—I did feel humiliated by the ass-chewing these anonymous people were giving me. My first reaction was: *I should never write again.* My second reaction was: *Well, I'll keep writing, but I'll stop trying to publish.* My third reaction: *What do I want for lunch?* In the moment, it seemed like a big, fat deal to be trash-talked on the Internet, but then I realized it didn't kill me. It didn't interrupt my life, it didn't cost me my job, and it didn't even stop me from writing. Not even for a day. It just made for a few minutes of stewing and that was it. That. Was. It. An hour later I was enjoying a chicken salad sandwich with a friend. Hey, hearing (and reading) bad stuff about yourself is never fun or easy. But take heart, knowing you will ultimately be okay.

5. Be the criticism you wish to see in the world. I don't claim to know sports all that well, but allow me to use this metaphor: The best defense is a good offense. You cannot avoid the criticism that is coming at you, nor should you—it's not only proof you are doing something substantial enough to criticize, but it's also the very thing that can make you even better. I find the best thing I can do is to be mindful of the criticism I give. I try to resist making catty comments, behind-the-back remarks, or mean-spirited gossip. I don't rip authors to shreds on Goodreads and I don't attack strangers on social media. I reserve criticisms for when I know the person is open and asking for feedback, and then I try to make it helpful and constructive. This does a couple of things: 1) it sets an expectation to others about how I would like to receive feedback, and 2) it helps me rest easy when I get a mean student evaluation or hear a super snarky comment about my work because I know I'm not guilty of being reckless with my criticism of others.

Even still, criticism sucks. Embrace that it sucks and try to remember that some things are simply unavoidable. Some critiques will be outliers; some will be helpful; perhaps all of them will be hurtful. But in the end, all you can do is be the best you can, learn when you can, and let the rest go.

• • •

Growing up, my favorite television show was *Dr. Katz, Professional Therapist*, an animated series on Comedy Central in the late 1990s. Come to think of it, I might have been a weird kid.

On the show, comedian Jonathan Katz voiced the therapist, while a variety of comedians' stand-up routines were repurposed as the ramblings of his patients. While it was by no means my first introduction to comedy, it did efficiently expose me to many of the most famous modern comedians. From that point on, I became obsessed with the profession.

What other profession demands high-energy performance, prompts brutal self-reflection, and allows hordes of people to anonymously judge one's professional ability on a routine basis? None that I can think of. Except being a professor.

I've never done stand-up in a dark nightclub for a crowd of drunks. But I regularly stand in front of a room full of people and try to get, and keep, their attention. For both the instructor and the comedian, the goal is to appeal to the greatest number of people in the audience. Both must entertain, challenge, and inform. Both try not to alienate anyone. And both must keep the audiences coming back—for the comedian, to pay the bills; for the instructor, to prepare them for the midterm.

But perhaps the biggest similarity between the comedian and the professor is the extreme way in which the professional is scrutinized. Scrutiny is both immediate and delayed, helpful and hurtful, and external and internal. As the comedian stands in front of the silent crowd, he can immediately tell he's bombing. Days later, he can read the critique in a critic's belabored review.

Every semester, a few weeks before final exams, college students get to evaluate their professors. They answer a series of questions in which they rank each professor on teaching style, course content, personality, and grading fairness (some open-access evaluation websites even let them rank us on hotness). There is also a comments section in which they can write any amount of feedback they feel is necessary. Student evaluations are a wonderful thing. They give students a great amount of voice and power over an experience for which they are paying. Professors can and do use this feedback to improve their courses, and the university can judge the effectiveness of the professors it employs.

On top of student evaluations, professors undergo peer evaluations, in which a fellow professor sits in on a colleague's class to observe their teaching style. Finally, professors submit numerous documents, including their student and peer evaluations, for an annual performance review.

Every class period is an immediate critique of my craft. Like the comedian, I must read the room. Some days, I walk out of class after dramatically dropping the mic, with the glint of sweat on my brow and the sound of uproarious applause following me out the door. Other days, I end class curled up under the lectern while students line up to have me clarify every single thing I had said during the preceding hour.

And when student evaluations come in, a week or so after the semester ends, there is the long-form critique of everything I did, said, or implied during the previous semester. The report includes a numerical value to show how I performed in all the areas evaluated. It also compares my score to those of other faculty members. The cold, hard data is easy to assess and accept.

But then there is the comments section. That's where the nuances of both the professional and the critic are exposed and more difficult to process. I typically open the comments section to find a screen full of dense text. The last time I did this, my eyes skimmed furiously to see negative phrasing, criticism, judgment, and disdain. I quickly closed the document and sat still at my desk. No matter how many students gave me good feedback throughout the semester, I can't help but view the end-of-term evaluations as the final word.

Looking at the life of a comedian, I know this feeling is common. Tig Notaro faces criticism of her sexual orientation from people in her hometown on *One Mississippi*. Amy Schumer joins in society's slam on her weight on *Inside Amy Schumer*. Even those who are deeply self-aware are still hurt by hearing what they already know. So, as I opened the comments section of my evaluations, I knew there would be no surprises. The good. The bad. I knew it all.

Fortunately, most every comment was positive, complimentary, and gracious. But then came those that weren't so glowing. There were comments from students who demanded a faster turnaround time on grades and desired a harder midterm exam. Wanted longer lectures. Needed me to talk slower. Talk louder. Talk softer. Talk less. Provide more PowerPoints, provide fewer PowerPoints, help explain what a PowerPoint is. Grade tougher. Grade easier. Stop assigning grades.

If a student ever called me mean—or heaven forbid, *boring*—I'd brush it off as radically unfounded. But when a student says that I sometimes don't explain certain things thoroughly or that I'm sometimes forgetful or disorganized, or points out some other part of my personality for which I already feel insecure, it hurts down deep.

I prefer to walk around thinking my flaws, weaknesses, and insecurities are hidden well beneath my Spanx and are my little secrets. So, when others who can see them so clearly point them all out to me, I feel vulnerable and exposed.

And yet, if I had to evaluate the students whose approval I'm vying for, I wouldn't have the nicest things to say about everyone. Like the student who was always trying to push back paper deadlines, the one who always tried to outsmart me, never showed up to class on time, or texted during every lecture.

From the array of insightful shows about the life of a comedian, lately I'm drawn to *Comedians in Cars Getting Coffee.* Just like *Dr. Katz,* Jerry Seinfeld exposes his audience to numerous comedians and their insecurities. Seinfeld begins every show with an in-depth description and visual inventory of a cool vintage automobile, while offering a candid and poetic reason behind its metaphorical representation of the comic he's on his way to pick up.

Numerous cameras harnessed in the car allow viewers to witness a genuine conversation between colleagues on their way to a coffee shop. The comedians discuss various topics, like child rearing and life on the road, intercut with beautiful footage of foaming milk and coffee pouring in slow motion. But the true substance comes from the scenes in which they talk about their lives in the field of comedy. In nearly every episode of *Comedians in Cars,* the guest will admit to having bombed in front of an audience when just starting out in the profession. They talk of the frustration and heartbreak of not getting laughs in the early years. It's the equivalent of adjunct teaching.

They talk of the constant feedback from the audience, the absurd need to please the crowd, and the humility— and resentment—that comes with that. And yet, the comedian and the professor are also the kind of professionals who can't seem to find their place in any other line of work. The constant performer.

Which makes me wonder whether, perhaps, both sought out a profession that continually puts them in a position to be judged. Is there some need they both have to be constantly evaluated? Do these people know their value only if it's constantly being measured? Maybe. But with any criticism, the comedian and the professor must remember to consider the source. A seasoned comedian surely knows this, and after a decade of teaching, I've learned it too. In the end, it's not what the crowd thinks that matters, but what the person standing in front of the crowd that does.

GIVE YOURSELF A BREAK

Self-criticism is a double-edged sword. On the one side, you have motivational speakers and perhaps those involved in multilevel marketing schemes, who say being hard on yourself ensures you'll go further and achieve more. Perhaps many of us believe that a little bit of self-torture is a strong motivator to do better. I see this line of thinking in my students and I certainly see it in myself. But current research contradicts this thinking. Kelly

Robinson from the University of Manitoba wanted to see if people associated self-compassion—the ability to be kind to and easy on yourself—as a negative trait. After all, if you give yourself a break, aren't you just lazy and unwilling to try harder? Robinson and her colleagues interviewed 161 people to gauge their attitudes toward self-compassion. The vast majority of those interviewed agreed that self-compassion is a wonderful thing that can make you a happier person. Even those who noted they did not practice self-compassion agreed that aiming to be more so was essential for well-being. Research backs up the notion that self-compassion reduces anxiety and helps people navigate negative life situations more easily. Interestingly, Robinson's study concluded that those who do not treat themselves with compassion when something goes wrong, do not because, while they conceded it would make them feel better, they believed it will only result in more negative outcomes. Perhaps it would make them soft or zap their ambition. Whereas, beating the shit out of yourself will naturally lead to a Nobel Prize.

Somewhere, somehow, we've decided tough love is the best for ourselves. We are quicker to give others a break, but much slower to pardon ourselves. I can't begin to count the number of times I've experienced this. Once, while I was sitting in the parking lot of a grocery store, a car pulled up beside me. Its door flung open and hit my car door with strong force. I jerked my head around to see who was responsible. A woman got out of the car, looked at me with no discernible emotion, and then slammed her door and walked off. My first thought was, *I wonder if I parked too close to the line.* Followed by my second thought: *Wait, I pulled in first!*

My friend Sarah calls this the guilty party mentality. It is a predisposition to blame ourselves before others, being quick to assume we're in the wrong and eager to assume we need to be better. And Sarah does not mess around. If she doesn't get a response back on a text quickly, she naturally assumes that the person she messaged must be mad at her.

One of my big pet peeves is how quick we are to beat ourselves up outwardly and openly. We complain about our weight, our hair, our lack of defined obliques. Someday I'd like to know what obliques are. (Okay, I just looked it up. It isn't what I thought and I'm absolutely not interested.) One subtle but common occurrence is when women post in appreciation of their significant others. I've lost track of the times women write, "Thank you for putting up with me!" It's subtle, but it's conveying she doesn't even think she deserves love. If you talk about yourself that way, it's that much easier for others to as well. Remember, people can only think and talk about you as highly as you are willing to think and talk about yourself.

But giving ourselves a break isn't easy. We have a lot about ourselves we want to change. Perhaps you want to be a little bit thinner, a little more successful, a little less negative, and a little more well-read. There is so much potential for self-abuse, when the reality is this: You. Are. Enough. Everything you are *right now* is enough. You already are everything you want to be. Something you want to change might be the very best part of you. Please practice self-compassion. Please give yourself a break. Whatever it is you are beating yourself up about, whatever things big and small you blame yourself for and are trying to change, relax your grip just a little. Praise yourself before you berate yourself. You might find your flaws, hangups, and worst habits have a way of solving themselves on their own.

• • •

Our older daughter came home from school one day with a splinter in her thumb. To her way of thinking, this was the most fascinating event that had ever happened in her life. She explained in great detail how she got the splinter on a piece of bamboo during craft time. She talked endlessly about how her friends had gathered around to share in her excitement and gawk at her finger. She gabbed on and on about her teachers' reaction to her splinter, and she boasted about how brave she was through it all. We could barely get her to eat dinner for all the talk of timber.

But as the night wound down and bedtime drew near, my husband and I informed her that we would have to take out the splinter. Her big saucer eyes blinked at us in confusion. We explained that we didn't want the splinter to cause an infection. Blink. We couldn't leave it in her finger. Blink. Blink. Then we reached for the tweezers. From that point forward, the most fascinating experience of our child's life turned into the most traumatic three days in our house.

Morning and night, we pleaded with our screaming child. We begged her to just hold still for one minute so we could pluck the log from her thumb. Instead of relenting, she would wail dramatically and crawl up to the highest point on the nearest piece of furniture. We asked for help from her teachers, but they are not legally allowed to pull out splinters. They stood quite firm on this policy; not a single teacher would bend to my attempts at backdoor bribery.

Finally, I had the bright idea to wait until our child was sleeping. We would sneak into her room with a flashlight and tweezers and gently extract the plank from her precious thumb. So that night, we bathed her, read her a story, put her to bed, and waited. When we heard her coherent talking shift into her sleep mumbling, we crept up the stairs. Jim carried the flashlight and I had the traumatizing tongs at the ready. But as we picked up her hand and turned it toward the beam of light, we saw a pink, vacant slit in her thumb. The splinter was gone. It had worked its way out on its own.

I often teach a research methods course designed to give graduate students the chance to learn about good research design and statistical analysis. The last time I taught it, I assigned a final project I'd never assigned before. Students would use the almighty scientific method to form and test a hypothesis on themselves. They would identify a problem in their lives—study habits, stress levels, social media addiction, and so forth—and determine an intervention that would alleviate it.

When I explained the final assignment in class, I was met with a sense of energetic hope, as if students would only be willing to improve themselves if it were for a grade. The assignment called for them to meticulously track numerous variables for a week, impose the intervention on themselves, and then track their progress for another week. They had to statistically analyze all the quantitative and qualitative data, then write up and graphically illustrate the findings. I urged students to think about something in their lives that they wanted to change; to give thought to a behavior or habit they felt was an obstacle to overcome.

On the night of the final presentations, a female student volunteered to speak first. She had experimented with reducing stress through daily meditation. She found that twenty minutes of meditation in the morning resulted in a statistically significant decrease in her stress-level scales. She even found that when controlling for the stress variable of Thanksgiving, meditation was still effective.

The next student also wanted to reduce stress and assumed that having an hour of downtime in the morning would help. She found that it did. Not only did she feel less stressed, but she also saw a spike in her productivity, especially on the days she spent her downtime away from electronics. A third student wondered whether his stress could be lowered if he listened to classical music for a set amount of time in the afternoon. His data was less conclusive, but the anecdotal evidence was promising.

Another student increased the amount of quality time he spent with his girlfriend to reduce the stress on their relationship. While he had mostly positive results, the girlfriend did not enjoy discovering, after the fact, that she was part of an experiment. One student went a week without any form of social media to see if it increased happiness. She had the most significant data to present, but warned that the withdrawal was difficult and relapse was inevitable. Another said she had incorporated thirty minutes of daily exercise to see if it helped her sleep quality. She found that she not only had a significant increase in sleep quality (as tracked by a sleep-monitoring device under her pillow), but she also stopped having headaches and lost five pounds. Another tried reading for fifteen minutes at night to see if it improved her sleep. It improved her sleep significantly, and she also realized she's a huge *Harry Potter* fan.

Student after student spoke excitedly about their experiments. While most students had success with their experiment, a few didn't. Those who didn't have success were reflective. Perhaps they measured the wrong variables. Others bemoaned a lack of rigidity with the intervention. Some wondered whether they computed their data incorrectly. The students seemed to understand the importance of experimentation and the power of validated results. Was it possible that this assignment not only conveyed the importance of research by personalizing it but also improved their lives? Assuming it had indeed, I posed one final question to the students: Did they continue with the intervention after the assignment was over? The response from each student was the same: lowered heads. Most everyone had resumed their behaviors as normal.

The morning after my daughter's splinter had magically worked its way out by itself, we awoke to the sound of her excited screams. "It's out! It's out!" she exclaimed, running around her room with her thumb triumphantly thrust skyward. We danced around with her, excited for her victory, and even more excited that that portion of our life—the one in which we pleaded with a screaming child to help her—was over. And it happened all on its own.

Reflecting on the splinter incident and in light of my students' research projects, I'm able to draw one substantial conclusion: Change cannot be forced. It can be feared. It can be embraced. But not forced. I suppose if my students really wanted to change a habit in their lives, they would. If they wanted to be on Facebook less, they'd log off. If they wanted better sleep, they'd get it. If they wanted a better relationship, they'd have it. Because bad habits and negative behaviors are like menacing obstructions buried deep beneath the skin. At some point, it needs to be removed. And there's plenty of research that points to the most probable outcome: It will work itself out on its own.

GIVE THOUGHT TO YOUR FORMATION

Consider the oyster. Each one is surrounded by endless grains of sand. (I realize it isn't grains of sand that form pearls, it's *parasites*. But sand is more poetic, even if inaccurate. So for the sake of the metaphor, just go with it.) To the outside world, it would seem that nearly all these grains of sand are created equal. They look to be the same color and size; nothing remarkable about any of them. And yet, one will get in. One grain will break the oyster's tough exterior and bury itself deep within the fleshy insides. As a defense mechanism, the oyster will lay down protective barrier after protective barrier, made of some gooey ick (don't overthink this), and those layers take shape and harden around that tiny speck. Over time, that small, seemingly unremarkable grain will be turned into something whole, something more precious and recognizable than the organism that made it. The pearl will overcome the oyster.

We don't get to choose those grains around us. We can't predict which grain will get in and irritate us down deep, activating our defenses and prompting us to spin it into something whole and nearly indestructible. As a parent, I delude myself into thinking I can control how my children perceive the life lessons I impart. For example, I want them to be able to express themselves. I want them to voice their concerns and to never be burdened by secrets. I carry out this lesson in a variety of ways. Now, maybe that lesson—which to them is just a grain among endless others—will be the thing that infiltrates. Maybe they will form into expressive children prone to transparency. But it's also possible the grain that will make it in is that time I screamed about the mud on the carpet. Perhaps they will form their identities around that tiny moment and cover their carpets and furniture in plastic tarps as adults.

I can see this in myself. My own mother and father set out to do lots of things as parents—they wanted independent, responsible children who weren't afraid to take risks in life. Check. But something they didn't realize, a grain of sand they didn't think would amount to anything, was a directive made to me as a young child.

I was just eight years old. Our family had endured a horrific car accident, and as I was being taken by helicopter to the hospital, my parents were told I had less than a 50 percent chance of surviving. My brother had been driving at the time of the accident. When I was released from the hospital four months later in a full body cast, my mother said—in what was certainly just projecting—that I needed to be sensitive to the fact that my brother was probably feeling guilty.

I think, as a parent now, I realize it was the exact thing to say and the correct stance to take. There was hurt all around—physical and mental—and it was important for them to take care of all the children as best they could. Blame was meaningless, so we needed to make sure it didn't get pointed in any one direction. But for whatever reason, my young, traumatized mind absorbed that grain and began to see my own pain and suffering as someone else's burden. So, I put so much effort and tension around it that by the time I was in high school, I had formed a perfectly whole identity around always worrying about the feelings of others above my own.

This doesn't mean I'm entirely selfless or that I put the *needs* of others above my own. But it does mean that I almost always defer to the feelings of others. I tend to feel at fault, guilty, or sometimes more concerned about what other people think than what I do. This is an exhausting way to live, but I built myself around the shape of that reality.

My parents didn't set out to make this the case, and they never could have predicted that fleeting moment would get absorbed down deep and covered over with layer upon layer of gooey ick. They wanted to help their family move past the tragedy while also making sure their son didn't feel the burden of what happened. I suspect—despite our best efforts—he turned that grain of sand into a pretty sizable mass.

What I'm saying is, many of us have allowed tiny grains to become the foundation of our formation. We don't always get handed a fair heap of sand, and unfortunately, we don't get to handpick the grains that break through our barriers. But there is a point at which we can look at the formation and question why we got this way. It's important to give some of your attention to the masses you've formed. What have you let fester into something that is now bigger and more substantial than you? Can you break down the pearl and see the grain for what it is? And if you can see the grain, can you reform yourself around it in a shape that feels less cumbersome to your insides?

• • •

Nearly eight years ago, on our honeymoon, I surprised my new husband with tickets to a play on the last night of our travels. We started our trip in California and then took a long train ride up the coast, making stops along the way and ending up in Portland. I wanted to surprise him with something, and when I saw that a production of *Guys and Dolls* was playing within walking distance of our hotel, I bought two extremely good—and pricey—tickets. This was only after a lengthy conversation with the theatre director, during which I asked for the experience level of the actors, the comfort of the seats, and the average temperature of the auditorium. I needed this to be perfect.

The night of the performance, I came out of our hotel bathroom wearing a little red dress to find him—as I had instructed him to be—in a nice suit. I was giddy as we walked out of the lobby and into the cold night, him still unaware of where we were going or what we were doing. We walked a few blocks and then, right in front of the theatre, I inhaled sharply. He looked up at the marquee and let out an excited laugh.

During the entire first act I kept my head turned slightly toward him, my eyes darting back and forth between the stage and his profile. We'd been married less than a month, but I felt like I could read him. I mean, I hadn't yet seen him recover from a vasectomy, and he hadn't yet seen me have an episiotomy, but I felt we knew each other pretty well. So I was mildly panicked that he looked so uninterested, so unimpressed—pissed, even— during the first half of the play. His brow furrowed, his mouth a simple and unmoving straight line. Had I just married a man who wouldn't even smile for a group of professionals singing and dancing their asses off?

When the lights came up for intermission Jim turned to me and exclaimed, "This is amazing!" I stared at him blankly.

"You're *liking* this?" I asked.

"What's not to like? This is great! Let's go get a drink."

And up he jumped excitedly, darting off in search of Scotch. I walked slowly behind him and wondered, yet again, if I had worried too much about what someone else thought.

A worry I've struggled with my entire life.

I recently watched an interview with a comedienne. She was recounting to the talk show host an explanation her friend had given as to why she is so funny and successful: because she doesn't care what people think. Ah, those brilliant and bold people who claim they don't give a damn what other people think. How refreshing. How empowering. How utterly full of shit.

To be successful at being funny, one must care deeply about the thoughts of others. That's how an audience works. And yet the ability not to care what others think continues to be a standard to achieve—by comedians and otherwise—as though it's some sort of universal compliment.

No successful woman (and certainly no man) would ever say, "I credit my success to the fact that I really care what people think." Nope. Because caring what others think is a really bad thing. We are supposed to go boldly in the direction of our dreams. And if we hurt people along the way, that's life! Go forth! Be selfish!

Now, as a person who cares deeply, immensely, about what other people think, I struggle to reconcile why it's such a bad thing. But I've been conditioned my entire life that the ultimate goal of a person is not to care what other people think. So I spend a lot of time trying to squelch my natural inclination.

As I said, my own struggles with what people think started young. But it hit its peak around junior high, naturally, and never really tapered off from there. In fact, in many ways, I feel more invested in what other people think now than I did in my adolescence. And that's saying something.

Let me be clear. When I worry about what others think, I'm not worried about what they think of me. I mean, I want my mother to think my hair looks good and my daughters to think I'm perfect in every way, but those thoughts don't consume me. I don't care if people think I'm smart. I don't need people to find me pretty. I don't even worry what people think about how messy I let my car get. Those types of thoughts don't touch me. And I worked hard to get to this place.

But I do concern myself with many, many other thoughts people have. I care what people are thinking. I naturally want people to feel heard and happy. I like to be helpful and useful, and if I know what people are thinking, I'm more likely to be both. Also, my professions—professor, writer, public speaker—demand that I care what people think. If my students aren't learning, readers aren't reading, or the audience is tuning me out, then I'm the one

responsible. So, whether by natural inclination or professional obligation, I give a lot of shits what people think.

Recently, I had a long advising session with a student.
After she left, I couldn't stop thinking about our talk. I
replayed the conversation over and over in my head for
the rest of the day. Was I too flippant about her problem?
Did I really listen enough to her emotions around it? Was
I pushing her in a direction she didn't want to go? Was
there leftover pesto in my teeth?

While I always feel very present when I speak with
students, I often find myself analyzing our conversations
later, always concerned about what they are thinking
and what they took away from our time, and wondering whether my advice was helpful. Many students get a
follow-up email from me to confirm they felt heard and
supported. You can't imagine how many of them say they
completely stopped thinking about our conversation the
second they left my office.

Beyond that, the concern over what people think infiltrates my parenting. Well, more accurately, the concern
over how much to care what people think.

My favorite trait in my older child, Lowery, is her
complete disregard for anyone else's time or energy. It's
also her most exhausting trait. But I marvel at how many
questions she can ask, how many items (food or otherwise) she can demand, and how many stories she can
tell in the span of one hour, let alone the entire day and
the past few years. Often, when she's in the middle of a
twenty-minute diatribe, I look at her and realize she does
not care one bit if I'm annoyed or tired or irritated. She

has things to say, answers to learn, and food to eat. What I've got going on is of no matter to her. And I can yell at her as much as my larynx will allow when she's in trouble, but she'll just shrug and keep on asking questions and demanding a snack. I often find myself coaching her to care a bit more what other people think. Me, in particular.

My favorite trait in my younger child, London, is her complete interest and fascination with how others around her react. It's also her most exhausting trait. But I marvel at how many hugs and affectionate pats she needs, particularly after she's been in trouble for throwing food at the wall. The only way to discipline London is to hold her in my lap and tell her in a soft voice, while stroking her hair and wiping her tears, that I would really prefer she not slap her sister in the face. And then I reassure her that I love her and that I'm not thinking anything but good thoughts about her. I often find myself coaching her to care a little bit less about what others think. Me, in particular.

I've seen my husband worry about what his parents think of his professional accomplishments. I've seen my students worry about what their current boss would think if they took another job. I know my friends worry what other mothers will think if they use bug spray containing DEET. But perhaps worrying about what our parents, our boss, or the other mothers would think gives us some accountability and context to our decisions, behaviors, and actions.

There's a danger in caring too much about what others think, sure, if it stops our ability to make decisions, endangers our relationships, or makes us behave in a way that conflicts with our principles. But the real danger is in the other extreme, when people really don't care what other people think. Because all that does is lead to the comments section of any news story on social media.

Caring about what other people think is a lovely thing. It's the purest form of empathy, and we should celebrate it a little more and shame it a little less. After all, it's the only thing keeping humanity in check.

During the *Guys and Dolls* intermission, while enjoying cocktails in the lobby, I told Jim how surprised I was to know he was enjoying the play. I explained how I thought he was hating it, that I had feared I had made a huge mistake in buying the tickets. He laughed and questioned why I would ever be worried about what he was thinking. I explained that his facial expressions didn't match what he was clearly feeling, and that I had spent the entire first half of the performance worried he wasn't having a good time.

To this day, if either one of us finds the other's expression not matching what they should be feeling, we demand the other stop "*Guys and Dolls*-ing" it. My students will tell you I have resting *Guys and Dolls* face when they are making presentations in class. My daughter says I have it any time she's asking a long series of questions.

Back in the theatre, among patrons milling around and drinking their last drops of cocktails, Jim leaned into me and said, "It's actually really great you cared enough to worry about what I was thinking."

Yeah. Of *course* it was. It's possibly one of the greatest human traits: empathy. And so what if that empathy kicks into overdrive sometimes? I *did* want him to have a good time. I *did* care what he was thinking. But after intermission and a cocktail, I really focused on the second half of the play, my head squarely facing the stage, my eyes unmoving. And I loved every minute of the performance.

But as for what Jim thought of the second half? I couldn't have cared less.

DON'T GIVE MORE THAN YOU OWE

In the ethics course I teach, I ask this question on the first night of class: Which matters more, intentions or outcomes? That is, are you deemed a good person based on what you intend with your actions or the actual outcome of your actions? Inevitably the class is equally divided on this question. Like clockwork, by mid-semester the students switch sides. This is a tricky philosophical question that plagues scholars. But when you break it down, intentions versus outcomes are at the root of how we choose to assess ourselves. Much of this comes down to what we think we owe others, ourselves, and the world. And what, specifically, are we willing to give?

What you believe you owe others is perhaps dragging you down. You owe your emails thoughtful replies, your texts swift responses, your boss your best work, your spouse your full attention, your children a safe and happy childhood, your neighbor a mowed lawn, your teeth a daily floss, your bank account a deposit, and your mother a call.

And yet, do you really?

Social contract theorists examine this question, specifically theorizing what we—as participants in society—owe one another. Granted, these theorists are arguing over how society should organize and function, but buried therein are societal norms that often make us feel overwhelmed by all we owe others (like thank-you notes and housewarming gifts!). John Locke and Thomas Hobbes are two social contract theorists who heavily influenced our constitution—which as we know, generally outlines what our government owes its people. You see, the debate comes down to understanding what values and rules govern how we decide what we owe one another. What is our moral obligation? Essentially, we tie up our actions toward others with our morality. No wonder we feel the weight of all those unread emails!

T. M. Scalon's book *What We Owe to Each Other* theorizes that what we owe others on a personal level is what moral equals can mutually agree on—meaning no side of the contract rejects the norm. But if that's the case, how did it get decided that men could mow without shirts while women would be arrested for doing the same? While my neighbor thinks it's fine, I certainly reject it! And yet the norm prevails. Men, you don't owe me a shirt; women, layer up.

Okay, so how much do ethical debates and America's early days influence your struggle to give all of yourself to everyone? More than you think. If the nation still can't agree on what the government owes its people, and ethical scholars can't pin down what our moral obligations are, how can you be sure you owe your friend a spa weekend? And why, *why*, are you spending so much damn time beating your head against the wall trying to be all things to all people?!? (I'm yelling this into a mirror, not at you).

You could argue that being a good person is often at the expense of being a free person.

Granted, my own political, social, and personal beliefs make me strive to be a good person. I want to contribute positively to my family, my students, and the world. But that drive often equates to feeling just a bit overwhelmed by what I have to *give*.

A few years into my job, I hit a wall with my teaching and what exactly it was I owed students in my class. It wasn't that they were asking for too much; I just thought I owed them more than I did. A colleague came into my office to find me with my forehead on my desk, as you do in the middle of a professional meltdown. When she asked what was wrong, I told her that I was running out of ideas to make each class fresh and interesting. She just looked at me, confused, so I continued: "I have all of these students for multiple courses. And I want each course to be a truly magical experience for them." I'll never get over how hard she laughed and, in turn, she will never let me forget that I said I owed the students "a magical experience."

"Meg, chill out," she laughed. "You don't owe them magic."

"What?" I asked. "Of course I do!"

"No, you don't," she replied calmly. "You owe them your time during class. That's it."

Now, she wasn't suggesting that I should merely sit at the front of the class clipping my toenails until our time was up. (Though that's certainly what I pictured when I heard her say exactly what I owed them.) She was pointing out that nowhere on paper does it say the students are owed a magical experience in class. All they are owed is: a class.

"Look," she said. "It's great to go the extra mile. It makes for an excellent classroom experience, it makes for a stronger graduate program, and it more than likely makes you feel pride in your craft." This acknowledgment of my impact was comforting.

"But just be clear to yourself about what you actually owe versus what you choose to give."

Since that episode—when I had wood grain imprinted on my forehead—I've been very careful to separate my true obligations from my voluntary contributions because it's not just at work that I bang my head against a desk. I want to give my kids amazing summer vacations. I want to share incredibly romantic date nights with my husband. I want to be completely available and present for my friends. I want to have an immaculately clean home. Now, I don't technically owe my kids a vacation, my husband a steak dinner, my friends a weekly happy hour, or my house a once-over with a vacuum. But so long as I'm aware I'm *choosing* to deliver more than I owe, I magically feel less pressure to do so because I can remind myself that I am in control of my gives. And I'm crystal clear to all involved that, even if I don't deliver on the outcomes, at least I had the very best of intentions.

• • •

The instant my lips sealed around the first bite of pumpkin pie I knew something was amiss. My mouth filled with bitterness. I glanced at my father. He was happily eating away, mere bites from finishing. I caught his eye. He shook his head, just slightly, as I started to say something. I looked down again at the pie. I didn't understand what was happening.

It was Thanksgiving. My mother had been up since four that morning; she always awoke early to prepare the turkey. She was an exquisite cook, and holidays were her time to shine. With the turkey in the oven, she worked on pies. My dad and I are the only ones in the family who like pumpkin pie and so she always, perhaps begrudgingly, made us one. But that year she had forgotten the most important ingredient in a pie made of gourds: sugar.

For years I carried the image in my head of my father eating every last bite of that disgusting pie. Narrowing his eyes at me to make sure I—a kid with a sweet tooth— didn't mention its terrible taste. I absorbed that moment as the touchstone of a good marriage: one selfless partner working hard to protect the other.

Many years later, when I met Jim, I knew I had found a man who possessed all the qualities I like: honesty, thoughtfulness, intelligence, and kindness. I wondered if he was the kind of man who would choke down a gross-tasting pastry I had made, and expertly mask his disgust while doing so. A couple of years ago—nearly a decade and two kids into our marriage—I realized that was exactly the kind of man he was.

That day was a busy one for me. My first book had just come out, and I'd been doing a series of talks and book signings. I was set to speak at a local library over lunch, just before the two graduate classes I had to teach later that day. Jim showed up to the book signing, smiling and intently listening along with the audience. As he hugged me after the event I asked, "Are you headed back to work?" He nodded. "Yes, very busy afternoon full of meetings," he said.

When I got home that evening I found it odd that his car was already in the driveway—he was never the first one home. I opened the door to find his dress shoes kicked off in the hallway, and him sitting on the couch wearing jeans. I knew something was wrong, but my mind couldn't work fast enough to figure out what. He stood up slowly, walked toward me, put his hands on my shoulders, and said, "I was laid off this morning."

That evening was fraught with concern. We hadn't been reckless with money, but we also hadn't prepared for losing more than half of our income overnight. We held each other and grieved. Should we take the kids out of daycare for a while? Should we sell the house? Did we really need two cars? Panic in one area of your life makes you believe all areas are vulnerable.

The next morning, Jim awoke as if he were getting ready for work. He shaved, showered, and left the house to meet with well-connected colleagues in the industry. His optimism served him well. He managed to swallow his bitterness and intentionally remained hopeful. In less than two months he was in a new job that was an even better fit, and a better package, than his old one. But I didn't quite feel relieved. There was still a bad taste in my mouth.

The morning he was let go, he was told within minutes of entering the building. He hadn't even turned on the lights in his office. Though we had been aware layoffs were happening in the company, his boss had assured him the week before that he was safe. After he left work, and before he came to my talk, he had taken a long walk to clear his head. I asked whether he had cried. He hadn't. I asked if he had felt scared. He had. I wanted to know everything he was thinking. I desperately wanted to share in his experience.

I kept having flashes to that day and how much fun I was having at the library, reading aloud from my book. How much I enjoyed answering questions from the audience. Or how great classes had gone that day. How I had flitted about at the lectern, talking passionately about the day's subject without a care in the world. How I had stayed late after class to talk with a few students. And how bad I felt about those feelings, and those extra minutes I took, when I thought about what my husband had been experiencing simultaneously. Those memories were forever altered.

Eventually, when I felt we both had emotionally stabilized, I told Jim how hurt I was that he kept the news from me the day he was laid off. He was surprised, but not the least bit apologetic.

"You had to give a talk," he shrugged. "And then teach two classes. Why would I tell you when there was nothing you could do?"

"Because it wasn't about there being something I could do!" I shot back. "It was about being part of the pain *with* you! Marriage is about sharing our life."

"It wasn't like I was keeping it from you forever. I just wanted to wait until it was a better time for you." He pursed his lips. "My intentions were good."

It wasn't a fight, but it was a divide.

I've thought more about that Thanksgiving when I saw my father choking down a truly terrible pie. His intentions were so clear to me, even in my youth: to protect his wife from something that would only bring her sorrow, something she couldn't change in the moment.

But only recently have I allowed myself to examine the other half of that story. After the meal, our family adjourned to the living room for coffee. I helped my mom clear the dishes from the table. She asked how the pie was. I stared at her, unsure what to say. She batted a hand in my direction and said, "Fine, I'll see for myself."

She plunged a fork down into the pie pan and scooped a sizable bite to her mouth. I watched uncomfortably as she jumped back in disgust and spit into the sink. She spun around fast, her face twisted in an expression that only now do I fully understand: regret. She marched into the living room and looked at my father sternly. "Why didn't you tell me about the pie!?"

Those few bites of pie were a fleeting moment in my parents' long and happy marriage. And with moments, just like ingredients, some matter more than others. My mother will tell you that intentions count for nothing in cooking. But my father would tell you that, in marriage, intentions are all we've got.

• • •

We've got to give if we want to get. So naturally, we assume that the more we want, the more we must give. That's not entirely accurate. You just have to give in a better, smarter way. Don't be a martyr about your dreams or your life. Be light, nimble, cunning. Give in the way a stealthy poker player gives: just enough to stay in the game and keep those around the table on their toes. But don't go throwing in all your chips thinking that's the only way to win the hand.

The Closer
for TACTIC FOUR

- **Give** a little of yourself to all the things you want. Even give a lot of yourself if you want. Just don't give all of yourself.

- **Accept** that the more substantial your contributions are, the more subject you are to scrutiny and criticism. In the end, it's a small price to pay.

- **Practice** self-compassion. You are enough.

- **Explore** the root of your reactions and behaviors. Change only that which you can no longer sustain. Keep the rest. It suits you well.

- **Remember** that in most cases, you technically owe very little. So give what you want without the pressure of believing it's due.

GETTING

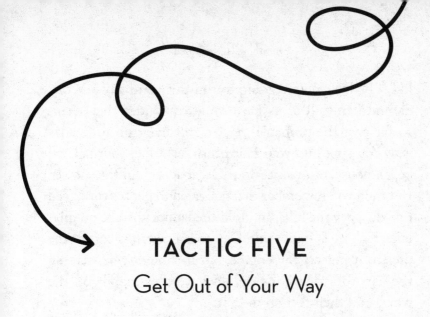

TACTIC FIVE
Get Out of Your Way

There will always be obstacles that stand in your way. Real, complicated, challenging obstacles. But *you* can't be one of them. You can't be the barrier between where you are and where you want to go. Yet many of us struggle to be the force that drives while not also being the force that stops. Understandably, negotiating for the life you want while not also caving to the first (second and third) feelings of doubt is a balance that is hard to strike. The best way to overcome your doubts, fears, anxieties, and insecurities is to defer to your delusions.

That's right. All of us have tiny bits of delusion that live deep within us. Some of you keep these hidden; you'd never tell another soul that you dream of winning a televised singing contest. Some of you wear your delusions like a badge; you are going to run this company one day, dammit! But all of us have some crazy idea that seems so far past the probable, yet we still hang on to it anyway. You sing into your hair brush, visualize your palatial beach house, or practice your Oscar speech in the shower. But then you remember that you need to get to work, feed the kids, pay the bills, and fold the laundry. Make no mistake, real life is important. Day-to-day work is part of the dream. It powers the engine, but it shouldn't be steering the car. Your delusions should have their hands on the wheel and their feet on the gas.

One of my favorite movies is Martin Scorsese's *The King of Comedy*. It's about a would-be comic named Rupert Pupkin, played by Robert De Niro, who kidnaps a famous late-night talk show host, played by Jerry Lewis, in an attempt to become a celebrated comedian. While watching, you can't help but look down on Rupert, with his unfounded confidence and delusional mentality. He believes if Jerry can hear his act, he will put him on his show where Rupert will be seen by millions and instantly become a star. So he sneaks into Jerry's limo after the show one night and begs him to have a listen. To appease him, and to get away from him, Jerry agrees to listen to the act if Rupert comes to his office. Every day, Rupert goes to Jerry's office and waits. When Jerry refuses to see him, Rupert breaks into his home to confront him. When Jerry kicks him out, Rupert kidnaps him, ties him up, and forces the producers of Jerry's show to let him do his set on the air as a ransom. After he does, Rupert is immediately arrested. In a few years, after his release from prison, there is so much built-up affection for the guy who kid-napped a star and manipulated his way onto television that he gets a multimillion-dollar book deal and his own television show. His delusions of grandeur brought him exactly that.

For as much rejection as you see this guy go through—and although every person he runs into thinks he's a co-lossal loser—you can't help but silently root for him. And it isn't as if Rupert isn't aware of what people think of him. He's not so delusional he can't feel all the rejection or hear all his detractors. He's just unwilling to accept other people's perceptions more than his own belief in himself. When he finally gets onstage, you realize he had worked hard on a compelling (and personally revealing) set. The point is, he had enough talent and had worked hard enough to do what needed to be done. But it took every ounce of his delusion to get him on the stage.

To get out of your own way, you must rely on your delusions to get you where you want to go. Once you're there, you can fall back on all the work and effort you've put into your craft—whatever that craft may be. But if you do not allow yourself to believe in the most unbeliev-able of your dreams, there will be no pressure or power propelling you there.

Many of our missed chances were because of some debilitating voice in our head. That voice was telling us either we weren't good enough, we weren't ready, or we didn't deserve it. If you really want to get something in life—big or small—you must believe that you are fantas-tic, ready, and worthy. Think of something right now that you want out of life. What does your delusion tell you? Perhaps your delusion is saying that you are going to be a world-renowned scientist who changes the way we view our world. Perhaps your delusion is sure that you're going to write the next great novel. Perhaps your delusion believes that you're going to change careers in your forties and finally feel professionally fulfilled. Maybe it's telling you that your soul mate is out there, your dream house is waiting for you, or your small business is going to turn into a national enterprise. Whatever it is, I know that you have already taken steps, consciously or unconsciously, to prepare yourself in case it does. You've taken the singing lessons, gone back for a master's degree, or put yourself out into the dating world. But you aren't letting your delusion sit in the driver's seat. You aren't letting your wildest dreams—which, by the way, are rarely unfounded or ridiculous—be the force that gets you to the stage where you can show off what you're made of.

GET OVER PERFECT

Perfection is a problem. Not a terrible problem, but a problem. You see, many of my students struggle with their quest to be perfect. They want to get a perfect score on every paper, deliver a perfect presentation, and ace the final exam. I see those as good goals—mostly. But perfectionism is a character trait that has two very strong dimensions—positive and negative—with polar-opposite outcomes.

In the past twenty years of psychological research into perfectionism, it's become clear that the character trait does come with some truly positive aspects. Psychologist

Randy Frost concludes that perfectionism has a variety of healthy and positive side effects. Those who strive for perfection tend to show more endurance, higher academic achievement, and even higher test performance. Basically, if you strive for perfection, you are going to get closer to the goal than if you don't. That's a great thing.

But the downside of perfectionism is what researchers Dunkley, Zuroff, and Blankstein call self-critical perfectionism—the dark side. This is when the strive for perfection leads to such vulnerability of mistakes and failure that it results in low self-esteem, feelings of unworthiness, and low self-efficacy. In this, you may give up if you think you have failed at something. And if anything less than perfect is failing, you're not going to get far.

Essentially, perfectionism can make you perform well but also might make you feel like shit. Researchers have worked for years to see if you can simply strive for one (positive perfectionism) without the other (self-critical perfectionism), with mixed results. In fact, a study out of the University of Kent built an experiment with undergraduate students to better understand the relationship between perfectionism and self-criticism and found they are highly correlated. Those who used perfection as a goal were able to set their sights on bigger goals, but they were also highly susceptible to losing confidence after somewhat minor setbacks. So a perfectionist is willing to go after a huge goal but feels completely defeated—and may even give up—if they don't reach that goal. If you think about it, this means perfectionists are most in danger of staying exactly where they are.

When it comes to perfectionism, here's what I've found from helping students (perhaps some of the most perfection-striving people of them all).

There Is No Target

Perfection has always been a confounding idea because who has the key to the ideal? I think students believe I have a lighted glass box in my office that contains the perfect paper, and when I sit down to grade their papers, I am comparing them to the paper in the box. Every aspect of their paper that doesn't hit the ideal results in points deducted. But that's not how grading works and it's not how life works. There is no ideal and therefore no *perfect* to strive for. Each paper starts with a 0 percent and, as I read, it receives more and more points. If you end up with an 89 percent, that means you built the paper up eighty-nine points from zero; not that you were eleven points shy of ideal. Assessing the quality of papers, like all things in life, hinges on context and content.

When I first started teaching at the college level, I thought I could somehow be the perfect instructor. For years I tried to emulate the best professors around me, which often meant doing things in the classroom—like two-hour lectures—that did not come naturally to me. After a while, I began to notice that the aspect of class I enjoyed the most was the one I was also the best at: facilitating discussion. A fellow professor I have long admired took me to lunch one day to ask me how I was able to get students to discuss and debate in class for hours. I looked at him quizzically and said, "That's easy. What I want to know is, how do you prepare and deliver lectures for hours?" He batted his hand as if I had asked him to teach me to tie my shoes.

Obviously, I believed the students all had an ideal professor in a glass box, and each class I stepped into compared me to that ideal. I eventually learned this wasn't the case. What happens is, I step into class and teach to my strengths, and students think, "Yeah, okay. I'll go with this." Instead of aiming for some arbitrary (and false) ideal, I decided to just steer into what I'm good at. Which means, above all else, I'm enjoying my time in the classroom. If students want a more lecture-heavy course, I know exactly where to send them.

Perfection Is Your Goal, Not Everyone's

I find my students are sometimes guilty of mistaking their quest for perfection as other people's problem. Maybe they push this on their coworkers, their group members in a class project, or, frequently, me. Inevitably, at the beginning of every semester, a handful of smart women approach me and say something like, "I need more clarity on everything in the syllabus. I'm a perfectionist and I need to get it right." This is problematic for a couple of reasons. The first is that these students believe that perfection is something achievable; the second is that they believe it's my problem to help them with it. And because they've started that narrative off with "I'm a perfectionist," I already feel concerned about how they will handle any feedback on papers or tests—feedback that is only meant to make them better.

When students tell me they are a perfectionist and aiming for a 4.0 grade point average (GPA) in grad school, I shudder a little. Think about it: If you enter something as challenging as graduate school and say, "I'm here but unwilling to be less than stellar," then you have stripped yourself of any growth. It would be like getting a record deal and saying, "I'm only willing to produce this album if I can be guaranteed it goes platinum."

I once received an email from one of my undergrad students that read, "I didn't get a perfect score on my test, despite feeling very confident and thinking I would get a 100 percent. This is going to impact my ability to get a 4.0, which will make it more difficult to get into graduate school later. Can we meet to talk about this?" Just reading her email I could tell she believed that her quest for perfection was now my burden to carry. She was approaching me as if I was the problem. She wasn't asking for additional tutoring or advice on how she could do better; she was only really focused on the fact that she didn't get what she felt she deserved. Her quest for a perfect GPA is something to which she was entitled, and I was the one standing in the way.

When we finally did meet I explained to her that her goal of a 4.0 was a completely worthy and solid one that I supported fully. But it should not supersede the actual purpose of education—to learn. And you only learn through the tried and true process of testing, failing, and trying again. To be clear, "failing" here is getting a B, or not being highest in the class. Failure is a scary word, but it's also relative and never final.

Perfection is an exhausting way to live, and when it comes down to it, it's motived by fear. It's okay—admirable even!—to set high expectations of yourself, so long as you remember that those expectations are your own. Don't throw your panic on your boss, kids, or teachers because they aren't granting you the achievement you desire. Chances are, you are exceeding their expectations of you and they are perhaps baffled by your dissatisfaction.

Consider Sustainability

People *over*estimate how hard it is to achieve something and *under*estimate how hard it is to maintain something. Remember when Michelle Pfeiffer gave all those inter-city kids A's in *Dangerous Minds*? Of course you do, it was a gripping performance. She gave everyone in her class the highest grade possible, a grade none of them had ever earned. And for a few minutes they all felt awesome because, come on, they were just given an A. But then she turned her chair around, sat on it backward, and rapped about how the tough part would be *keeping* it. Yeah. That's the thing about perfection. What happens if you ever achieved it? How would you maintain it?

A good friend of mine lost more than eighty pounds. Though it wasn't an easy journey, she was highly motivated during the weight-loss process, even through some tough plateaus. When she finally hit her goal weight she commented to me that the most exciting part—even more than her new and amazing figure—was the process of losing weight. She had a goal, motivation, and energy behind it. But once she achieved it, she found keeping herself at that weight was so much harder than getting to that weight.

This doesn't mean you shouldn't strive for a good grade, or to lose weight, if that's what you want. But what I am saying is that if you are currently working yourself tirelessly to achieve a nearly impossible standard, have you considered how much harder you'd have to work to maintain it? Is that the best use of your time and energy?

If I can devote an entire Saturday to cleaning, I can usually get our house as orderly and spotless as humanly possible. But keeping it that way? Forget it. So I don't strive for a perfectly clean house because for one thing, spending that much time on cleaning is a waste of a good weekend. For another, I can't (or refuse to) put in all the effort to maintain it at that level.

Instead of seeking perfection, find your level best. Have high standards, not impossible ones. Strive for a level that stretches you and that you work hard to achieve, but not one that kills you to keep yourself at. For my friend, it was about ten pounds heavier than her initial goal weight. For my house, it's getting it clean enough that I won't be embarrassed if someone stops by, but not so clean *Architectural Digest* would want to put it on the cover.

Excellence is different from perfection. One can be achieved and maintained. The other cannot. Strive for excellence. Strive for your personal best. But for the love of Pete, give up on the quest for perfection. And while I feel this gets said a lot, I'm going to say it again for good measure: Done is better than perfect. I can't begin to count the number of times students have asked for an extension on a paper so they can have more time to perfect it. But I've yet to see an instance where the student's extra effort for perfection made up the points deducted from turning it in late. Understand there is no universal target, only your personal excellence. So whatever it is you are working hard for, simply do your best, and then let it go.

• • •

When I was on the verge of completing kindergarten, I was scheduled to take a test measuring my readiness for the first grade. My mother accompanied me into a small room where the test proctor sat at a table with nothing on it but a single piece of paper and a pencil. I sat down, my mother beside me. On the paper was a circle. I was instructed by the proctor to draw a face.

I picked up the pencil and, on the far side of the circle, drew one eye. The proctor looked pleased. My mother beamed. Then I put the tip of the pencil on the outside edge of the circle and drew what appeared to be a triangle. The proctor fidgeted. My mother remained calm. Then I finished by placing the pencil back inside the circle, and, near the edge, drawing half of a smile. I put the pencil down and looked up at my mom. She was pleased.

The proctor was not.

I had drawn a face in profile. The proctor explained to my mother that wasn't the intent of the test. The test was to see if I could place two eyes, a nose, and a mouth within the circle in an arrangement that would best represent a face. She picked up the pencil and asked me to erase what I had drawn. My mother extended her hand to gently intercept the pencil. She explained to the proctor that her instructions never specified the face had to be forward-facing. The proctor said if I wasn't able to complete the test as it was intended, she would not recommend me for the first grade. Whatever transpired in the room after that is still a bit fuzzy. All I remember was my test being taped to our refrigerator at home and, in short order, starting the first grade.

School is nothing if not the push and pull between conformity and individuality.

In the classroom I'm always asking my students to both fit a mold (everyone must be present, engaged, and participating) and to be themselves (bring in your own experiences, express your individual opinions). Everyone gets the same paper assignment (same page requirement, structure, and citation guidelines), but I want them all to be creative and distinctive within that assignment (pick a unique topic, bring in your own point of view).

Now that our oldest is in school, I see the push and pull between conformity and individuality coming strongly into play. But, much like my first-grade entrance exam, I also see the push and pull between parental involvement and independent growth.

Lowery came home recently with a homework assignment: an outline of a turkey with instructions to "disguise it" so it wouldn't get eaten on Thanksgiving. I didn't give this assignment much thought. It was buried within the abundance of papers that come home every day, so I glossed over it. Jim, however, did not. He always carefully reads each piece of paper and makes notes of deadlines in our family calendar. Unbeknownst to me at the time, this turkey project was heavy on his mind.

The night before the turkey project was due, we had to attend an unexpected work-related event. As I gave dinner instructions to the babysitter, Jim told Lowery she would need to complete her turkey project. He explained that she had to disguise the turkey, and he left her with her bucket of markers, glitter, and stickers. She nodded with the confidence only a five-year-old can possess, and off we went.

That evening, we got home in time to put the kids to bed. We read to them, giggled with them, talked to them about how their evening had gone, and tucked them both in with a kiss. Back downstairs I heard Jim let out a groan. When I walked in to see why, he was holding up Lowery's turkey project. It was the turkey completely colored over in brown marker.

I let out a laugh and clapped. "That's awesome!" I exclaimed. He looked pained.

"She can't turn this in," he said.

"Why not? It's hilarious. And clever."

"No, no. This isn't the intent of the project. Kids are meant to disguise the turkey."

"Yeah, well, that's a tough concept for a kindergartener to understand. She clearly took it to mean 'hide' and that's what she did," I said, still laughing as I admired it.

The next morning, as we rushed around to get the kids ready, Jim asked to talk with me alone in the kitchen.

"I can't let her turn in that turkey," he whispered, pulling at the knot in his tie.

"Sure you can," I said.

"No, seriously. We failed as parents on this."

"Excuse me!?"

"Meg, this was supposed to be a family project and we let her do it on her own. She's going to get laughed at."

"Laughed at, why? And by whom?"

"I just know how this is going to go. Parents are going to have helped their kids, and they are going to be over-the-top masterpieces. And hers is, well, a blob of brown."

"Hey now. She hid the damn turkey. You can't eat what you can't see! Besides, we don't parent for other parents."

"Meg, just let me ask the teacher for another turkey."

"There's no need. She did the assignment and it's great."

At that point Lowery walked into the kitchen. "Are you talking about me?" she asked. It was time for school. That evening, when I arrived home after teaching my class, Jim seemed more relaxed. The kids were in good moods as we put them to bed. Back downstairs I asked, "Good day?"

He smiled and held up a piece of paper. On it was a turkey, colored to look like a purple unicorn, complete with drawn-on horn and tail.

"What's going on here?" I said, my smile fading.

"Well, the teacher forgot to send home another Turkey in her folder—"

"You asked for another one? I thought we agreed—"

"And so I just took the brown blobby one, held it up to the light, and traced the outline of the turkey. Then I made a photocopy of it so it would match the others."

"This is insane, Jim."

"No, you don't understand. When I got to school today I saw what the other kids were turning in. One turkey was disguised as Superman, with a cape glued on it."

"Okay, well that was clearly a parent…"

"Another was a snowman made of cotton balls."

"Yeah…okay…I get it, but—"

"One had a beaded necklace glued to it. I think it was Elizabeth Taylor."

I looked back down at the purple unicorn. How meticulously Jim had traced the turkey outline through the original dark brown blob. I looked in admiration at the twisty horn he had drawn and the thoughtful way Lowery had colored various shades of purple on each of the turkey's feathers. I sighed and smiled up at him without any more to add.

A few days later, Jim and I met for lunch. Having not spoken about the turkey again since he proudly handed it over to the teacher, I couldn't disguise my concern any longer.

"Can we talk about the turkey?"

"Sure…"

"What the hell was that all about?"

That turkey was the first time—aside from "who is going to change the next diaper"—that Jim and I were at odds about a parenting choice. We spent that lunch break hashing out what exactly had happened, why I was so reluctant to get involved, why he was so obsessed with being involved, why he took charge before we had agreed on a plan, and why I was resistant to push conformity. On and on it went until by the end of the lunch a strange thing happened: We completely switched sides of the argument.

"I think you're right," Jim said, shoulders slumped. "I basically did the assignment just so she matched the other kids. I didn't let her own it."

"Nope. I'm an idiot," I sighed. "It was intended to be a family project and I'm just sensitive to those mandatory parental involvement assignments. It undervalues all the ways we are involved. I was obviously projecting."

"No, I was projecting."

"No, you were being an exceptional father."

"Nope. You were the one modeling good parenting."

Like any good argument, we both left still on opposite sides of the issue and more confused than ever. As if we think this one assignment sets the tone for our child's entire education.

That day in the testing room, when I was in kindergarten, my mom let me be who I was and rejected any awareness or pressure of conformity. And she stayed right next to me so she could fight for my independence when needed.

In one artistic exercise when I was five years old, I learned what my goal was and what the goal of my parents was. Maybe the turkey project was a lesson for Lowery, too. But what exactly did she learn? Does she know to strive for distinction within the conformity? And does she know her parents are there to step in *only* in defense of that? Here's hoping.

I take heart knowing a new folder filled with assignments is surely on its way. With it comes another chance to show her what we're made of and another opportunity for us to figure out where exactly our place is in our child's education and in her life. Whatever our place may be, I know sometimes we will need to make our efforts abundantly clear and, other times, keep them expertly disguised.

GET FOCUSED

There are generally two types of students (and therefore, perhaps two types of people): those who have lots of big plans and know exactly what they want to do with their lives; and those who have no real idea what they want to do, save for a few various interests. The commonality between these two types of people is that neither knows exactly where to start. Those who have big goals and lots of them don't know how to take a bite out of the mass. Those who are unsure what they should do next are waiting around to figure out which way to go.

Focus is key. You need to be mindful of what you focus on. For starters, let's address one thing you should *never* focus on: your enemy. Maybe your current enemy is a family member, a colleague, or a database at work you just can't seem to master. But you can't focus on this enemy because your enemy is always evolving. It's a sneaky shape-shifter. If you focus too much or too long on your enemy, you will find that it will simply reappear in another form the moment you defeat it. You shouldn't have the same enemy that you did in high school, after all. If you do, darling, that's on you.

The first course I ever taught at the college level was difficult because of one problematic student. I believed that the key to my success would be in the following semester's class, which I knew this student wasn't in. But care to guess what happened the next semester? There was a different problematic student. For over a decade I've had a difficult student in every course I've ever taught. For years I thought I could achieve my highest level of teaching if I could just outpace this problematic student who kept reappearing in different forms. But I eventually realized that this student was going to take on many forms every semester and my focus should never be on that, but rather on the many other aspects of teaching I can directly impact. So now, I just factor a problem student or two—as well as varying classroom temperatures and hiccups with technology—into each class I teach.

A lot of energy gets eaten up by these "enemies." (I once spent a day stewing over—and trying to rally my colleagues around—our coffee maker at work because every pot tasted burnt. I may or may not have missed an important meeting because of it.) But if people release themselves from thinking about the enemy, they suddenly free up a lot of energy they can allocate more effectively. So now what?

1. Focus on what you can improve. Notice I didn't say "focus on what you can *control*," mostly because you can control a lot of things that could result in negative outcomes. You can control what you eat, so you may decide to indulge in ice cream sandwiches round the clock! You can control your work, so you may decide to half-ass it all day. You can control how you spend your time, but you may decide to fill it with booze and drugs, and ice cream sandwiches. The point is, don't stop at just what you can *control*; focus instead on what you can improve. It gives you a more direct and positive sense of purpose. If you can't improve it, you aren't in control of it anyway. And if you are in control, why the heck wouldn't you try to improve it?

2. Focus on the process, not the outcome. This is counterintuitive, I realize. After all, people are always saying, "begin with the end in mind." Goal-setting is productive; having that goal hijack your every move is not. It's not that you can't have a big, juicy goal in mind. You just can't get stuck on every detail of it. I had a student apply for our program because she really wanted to be an executive director of a nonprofit (she even had a specific nonprofit in mind). With her mind set so hard on the outcome, I wondered whether she would enjoy the process. When I asked, a few semesters in, she said, "Well, I'd really like to take classes in another subject area—maybe public policy—but I can't imagine that will help me get the executive director job." I suggested she try out just one class in a different field. After that one class, she became so interested in the subject, she started taking more and more courses, eventually graduating with an entirely different concentration than she came into the program to study. And guess what? She *still* got a job as an executive director, with an agency that was thrilled about her diverse educational background. The point is, you can't control (or improve) the thoughts or potential wants of others (future employers or otherwise). So have a big goal, but don't let it dictate your every move because you think the goal requires it. Focus your energy on enjoying the process. That will more than likely lead you to exactly where you want to go, and no matter what, you'll have a good time along the way.

3. *Focus on the grains.* Many (most?) problems in life, at work, and in love are systemic and can often be easily solved if you're willing to explore what's at the root. I addressed this concept once at a talk I gave to a company run—and staffed entirely—by women. I posited that larger problems can almost always be alleviated by tinkering with the most minute issues. I talked the group through some organizational examples geared toward their industry. A woman in the back raised her hand and said, "Okay, but can you help me with my problem of managing my crazy, chaotic life?" Amused and delighted she was making a management issue more personal, I asked her for more information. She said, "I live in absolute chaos. I'm married, with a two-year-old, I've gone back to grad school, and I work here full-time. I'm apparently a masochist!" The crowd laughed, and I did, too.

When the room quieted down, I said, "It sounds to me like at the most granular level, your problem is the way you talk about your life; the way you *see* your life. I haven't even met you and you introduced yourself with words like 'crazy,' 'chaotic,' and 'masochist.' I'd venture to guess that you are in love with your life—however busy it is. That you are in a job you love, raising a kid you love, and are *voluntarily* going back to school." She nodded dramatically in agreement. "Then perhaps the grain to focus on is the way you view and talk about your life."

You are only one person with only so much to give. Chances are you don't need to focus *harder* on something; you just need to focus *better*. Budget your focus more efficiently. Take it away from the enemy and put it into better things. Take my own example, of saving and growing an academic program, as a study in focusing on the craft, on what I could improve, and on the smallest details.

• • •

When I was offered my current job I was told of the challenges that awaited me. I was there, on the branch campus of a major state university, to essentially save a dwindling graduate program.

To their credit, the administration graciously gave me the freedom and creative license to drive the direction of the program on the branch campus. This meant that important people within the university system were interested to know what my strategy was going to be. What was my overall plan for recruitment? What specific sections of the professional market would I try to corner? Did I need a budget for billboard ads and click bait?

The truth was, I didn't have a plan. I didn't have a strategic vision or a recruitment strategy coming into the job. All I had was a goal: grow and strengthen the program. And given how small the program had become and how new and green I was, this was a big goal. I decided to start with a simple idea, which was born more of necessity than wisdom: take care of the people in the room.

On my first day on the job, I came into a room with six students in it. They were all I had. I was fearful they would also leave the room, so I set out to give them everything I could. I listened to their concerns, wants, desires in a program, and the classes they were most interested in taking. I scheduled those classes, created assignments around their interests, and booked guest speakers to satisfy their curiosity in certain areas. I built up every inch of that program around six people in a room.

Those six students graduated a year later. They are among the most ambitious and brilliant people I've ever met. Some went on to take important, change-making jobs in the community. Others were promoted within their fields. One went as far as Africa to work with a nongovernmental organization focused on women's health. But every single one of them did another valuable thing: They talked about their experience in the room. Before long, others were applying, and soon I had a few more people in the room. On and on it went, until a couple of years later when the room was overflowing. Because of one simple strategy, a nearly defunct program on campus grew to a flourishing and sustainable program with a constant stream of new students.

I find that big goals cause people great anxiety. I push my students to always live with a bit of that anxiety because if they aren't feeling it, they aren't dreaming big enough. But those big goals often paralyze people before they even get the chance to make progress toward them.

Many students come into class on the first day worried about their final grade. Many prospective students worry about what they will do with the degree after they graduate, before they've even decided to apply. The deal is, everyone has a goal. A *big* goal. Sometimes many big goals. But they are a bit fuzzy on the plan. So, here's the plan: Start with the people in the room.

Some of my most productive days end with me getting nothing done. I have an open-door policy, which means students can, and do, frequently stop by. While it's difficult to ever make much progress grading papers or returning emails, it puts the power in the hands of those who enter the room. Once they sit down in front of me, they become my focus.

That isn't a terribly efficient way to run a day. It's often slow work, and I wonder whether I spent my time wisely. But the truth is, taking care of those in the room *is* the work. An hour with one current student seems to make a far greater impact than talking to twenty potential students at a recruiting event.

The room is where the most important work is done. I've sat in plenty of meetings with colleagues where the laptop divides us—remotely sent messages are the priority in the room. Or people are distracted by what's just outside the room—the next meeting, a pile of paperwork, unread emails. Or they forget to really listen to the thoughts of those closest. Or worse, they don't get consensus, buy-in, or excitement from those around the table before rolling a plan outside the room.

In class, I have a reputation for being a Luddite. I don't allow phones or laptops, which is tough on the students because they want to work all the time. They want to write while in class, get started on the next project, or start researching for the next week's assignment while the class is discussing this week's assignment. And they sometimes look at their house on Google Earth.

I get it. That's how we are built to think, that somehow activity is productivity, and that productivity is the only way to achieve our goal. But when my students are without distraction and are focused solely on the other classmates in the room, everyone learns more. They have a better experience and they are way more prepared for the next week's assignment.

When I get home at night I often feel the pull of work: emails from my students and grading. Or I feel the tug of a social life I currently can't quite sustain: texts for a happy hour or an invitation to a dinner. But when I walk in and see my kids and my husband, that's the room I must focus on. One of my big goals is a happy family life with lasting relationships. So my oldest's histrionics and my youngest's requests for a hug are what's in the room.

This isn't easy, especially for someone like me who always wants to be working toward a goal, growing, improving, excelling, inspiring, and creating. And at any point in time something somewhere on Instagram needs my double-tap.

But progress is, by its very nature, *progressive*. So start with what's right in front of you.

To my students I say, don't worry about the final. Start with the current assignment. Enjoy it. Work hard on it. Excel at it. That's going to be the thing that earns you the grade you want in the end, and the building block of a graduate experience you want. Which is the experience you'll need to achieve those big, anxiety-inducing goals. To the university, I said I would be able to deliver on their big goal, but only if I started small. And that meant just six people in a room.

Big goals start with small plans.

Make your goal as big as you can imagine it. But start by grasping at those things within your reach. Start with the people in the room. Focus there. And like a rock diving deep into the water, ripples will infinitely extend from the impact.

Impact the room. Whether it's a classroom packed with bright, young minds; a meeting room full of colleagues; an office with one student needing help; or a living room alive with chatter, take care of the people in the room.

Perhaps most important, don't forget to take note of the times you walk in a room and find yourself completely alone.

And take care.

TAKE STOCK OF WHAT YOU'VE GOT

Sometimes in our quest for what we want in life, we miss what we've already got. We may struggle with our ideals when we see them play out in reality. Almost all of the students I speak to have a million images in their head of the things they want to do, create, or achieve in their lives. Maybe it's a great career, a wonderful marriage, or a litter of kids. Many times, it's *all of those things*. So I often talk with students who have a beautiful set of pictures in their minds about their lives, but they cannot see those pictures clearly. They have to squint to make out all the details. And so, when their images become reality, they don't recognize them.

My student Jack reached out to me in a panic. He was feeling extremely down, saying he was at a crossroads in his career. I met him for coffee one afternoon on campus. Jack is a grant writer at a well-respected nonprofit agency that works on issues of race and social justice—causes that are close to Jack's heart. When I asked him what the issue was, he explained, "This just isn't how I pictured it." When I asked what exactly he had pictured, he toyed with his coffee cup, let out a sigh, and said, "My whole life I've wanted to make a difference, especially around issues of race. And look at me. I'm just a lowly grant writer who isn't doing anything to make a *real* impact."

I let Jack talk. He kept going about how he had this image in his head of the person he thought he would be: a change-maker, a fighter for social justice, a warrior. When he fell quiet, I asked, "Jack, aside from wanting to make an impact on race relations, what excites you?" He explained that he loved creative endeavors, especially writing. He wished he had more time to write creatively, or even just an op-ed piece for the paper. I nodded and asked, "And how much money do you think you've brought in during your years as a grant writer for your agency?" He leaned back and looked up at the sky while he tallied in his head. "More than $5 million," he said as his head tilted back down to meet mine.

Here's a guy who wants to make an impact. Aside from that, he's creative and enjoys writing. So, let's frame the picture: Jack is getting paid to write, and while doing so he brought in millions of dollars for a cause he believed in. When I explained this to him, he said, "How the hell did I not see that?" He didn't see it because sometimes, if a picture isn't framed, we can't see it fully. A frame gives our eyes a chance to see the edges around our image; it provides the definition.

I hear this kind of talk a lot. I hear it from students who, like Jack, believe their career isn't what they thought it would be. Or a new mom who isn't feeling like she's quite the mother she imagined she would be. Or a newlywed who is unclear if marriage will be like she hoped. Images in our head are blurry and sparkly and mystical, but they lack definition. So when we see them in reality, we can't focus on the image if it isn't framed.

I think in my own life, and in the lives of the students I advise, the soft-focus image in our head is easy to go after but hard to see when it appears in full form. We imagine the great career, the perfect spouse, the darling children, and the amazing person we want to become. But even when it happens, we can't see it.

Karen Christopher conducted an interesting study at the University of Louisville in 2012. She interviewed nearly fifty working moms to understand how the women constructed the ideals of good mothering. Specifically, did they believe good mothering was being incredibly hands-on and personally taking care of all aspects of parenting? Or did they find good mothering involved delegating some parenting responsibilities to their partners and childcare providers? Working mothers with helpful spouses saw good mothering as delegating some of the responsibility, but still having control. Mostly, they saw this delegation as good mothering because they also saw the personal benefits of their careers, benefits beyond the financial one. The results of this study show a change in mothers from earlier studies on this topic. Essentially, the researcher concluded, mothers have reframed what the image of "good mothering" is. And in this case, mothers have seen that the images of their valuable career *and* their desire to be good mothers can exist within the same frame.

You can have the image of your dream career—you can earn the degree, get the interview, negotiate a great salary—but your image doesn't contain the true day-to-day details: the boring meetings, the annoying coworker, that moldy thing in the common-area fridge. Those fuzzy images don't clearly show all the times the guy down the hall hits "reply all" on an email. That doesn't make the image wrong; it just makes it unclear. Now, when the image starts to come into focus and get framed by reality, that's when you know your dream has come alive. That's right, the never-ending email chain *is* the dream! Getting to flesh out the image, even with all the flaws, is the exciting part of living out your plans. But you can't misinterpret those sometimes daunting dimensions. Don't use them as an excuse to erase your images. Use them as an opportunity to reframe the picture. Take me and my own images of motherhood for example.

• • •

It started with a simple question: "Is tomorrow picture day at school?" The first few words of the question were pronounced innocently enough, but by the time I bit down on the final word, my voice had risen in panic.

The weekend is always a blur of temper tantrums, snack dispensing, and ass-wiping. As the chaos was trying its hardest to calm down one Sunday evening at 5:45 p.m., a thought hit me while I was cooking dinner: Monday was picture day at my child's daycare center.

Letting out a gasp of panic, I quickly turned off the stove, ran into the living room to find Jim, and blurted random words like "pictures," "tomorrow," "no time," "clothes," and on and on as I dashed out the door and into the pouring rain.

With tires trying to get traction on slick streets, I steered the car a block away to a store I knew was open for just fifteen more minutes. I raced inside, drenched, my eyes darting across the racks and shelves looking for something, *anything*, that coordinated. I instantly saw two dresses and let out a small yelp as I realized they were both 50 percent off. I pawed at the articles of clothing, desperately searching for the corresponding sizes, and raced to the counter just as the manager was trying to lock down the cash register. I helped him stuff the dresses into a bag and crumpled it tightly under my arm as I hunkered down to run out again in the torrential downpour.

At home, chilled and soaked, I dried off with a towel my husband handed me, then I finished preparing our meal. I was shaking from the adrenaline, unable to calm my racing heart. I continued cooking while fuming about my forgetfulness. That night, after the kids were put to bed and the dishes were being swished and swashed within the dishwasher, I explained to Jim—who was far too kind to ask—why the hell I ran out of the house just to get two dresses for picture day at school.

I described how a week earlier, when I had heard about school pictures, I had been excited to get the girls new dresses. London, regrettably—though economically— has been in hand-me-downs her whole life, and Lowery, regrettably—but proudly—tears holes in every pair of pants I buy her. And while accessorizing my children is certainly fun for them and for me, I rarely get around to it much anymore. Unless there are pictures to be taken.

The next day, Jim dropped the girls off at school, all pressed and coifed. He texted me later to say it was clear a few other parents had forgotten about picture day as well, so I was in good company. After that, my phone was lit with texts from fellow mothers remarking how adorable my children looked, but dammit, they had completely forgotten about picture day and, oh well, that stained T-shirt and muddy pants will make for a good story when the kids are older.

Even though I felt I had barely squeaked by with an army crawl across the finish line, other mothers were declaring me an all-out victor. And they were forfeiting. That part of motherhood—that solitary panic and hustle, racing against a clock that doesn't tick—is the part I really, *really* don't like.

I've been asked a lot lately whether I like being a mom.

This is a fair question. It most often comes from my well-meaning young students who want children someday. Or, sometimes, by my own child when I'm in the middle of fighting with her over bath time.

But there's something about the question that is problematic. My obvious and immediate response is one of great enthusiasm, for I must not let anyone think, even for a second, that I don't love being a mother. Because thanks to my generation's overkill parenting style, we all must be constantly proving we love our children—no one will just assume.

The weird part about being a mother is that it is treated very differently from the other roles I play in my life. I have never been asked whether I like being a daughter or a friend. I've never even been asked whether I like being a wife. But the answer to that question is that it is *super* contingent on it being in relation to Jim. If he up and left, I doubt "being a wife" would be a priority of mine.

The point is, motherhood is contingent on the child. I like being Lowery's mom and I like being London's mom. But it's a funny thing to even ask, about as funny as asking whether I like being a human. But motherhood is a role that seems to miraculously float somewhere off in the distance. We put motherhood on a separate plane in time and space and watch it from afar. We make it a role to which one aspires, achieves, and perfects.

When I was ready to have kids but had yet to see a blue line on a stick, I wanted to have other mothers tell me how amazing it is. I wanted to hear about the cool club I was desperate to join and how much happier I would be once I was in. Only to find out, once I was in, it involves a lot of temper tantrums, snack dispensing, and ass-wiping. And that's just not the kind of under-the-nails shit you want to unload on a bright-eyed young woman excited for motherhood.

But the thing is, motherhood isn't all that bad. It's just all that glorified.

As young girls, we talked about being mothers one day. I can't remember what my general opinion was on having children, but I sure played "house" a lot with my friends. From an early age I saw that motherhood was easy so long as my children were as quiet and well behaved as Cabbage Patch dolls. And because dolls don't move or talk or shit (well, they didn't in my day), it was easy to see motherhood as a monologue, not a dialogue. Motherhood was something to be done *at* a child, near a child, and/or around a child. Not *with* a child. So began the process of seeing motherhood as a role I would conquer, not as a relationship I would have.

Before I was pregnant I was really excited about a whole host of motherly activities, despite never having any experience with them. One aspect that excited me was the prospect of my children going to school. The thought of being the homeroom mom, or the mom who always had coffee for the teacher, seemed like something I would not only enjoy, but somehow be extremely skilled in.

But, now that I have a child in kindergarten, I find myself often resenting the homeroom mom who always has coffee for the teacher. Mostly because she's always consuming the teacher's attention at dropoff and the other parents have to fight to get a word in. Six weeks into the school year a well-intentioned mother sent an email to all the classroom parents with the task of collecting money for the teacher's birthday present. Her email began with three paragraphs explaining why she thought our teacher was great and why we should get her a gift. This email seemed to assume we didn't know all of the reasons the teacher was great and it put every parent in defense mode. So as not to appear as if they disagreed with her assessment of the hard work and dedication of our teacher (or hadn't already bought her a birthday gift!), nearly every single parent responded with effusive comments by *replying all*. If I teach my children anything, it will be about the rare instances in which replying all (or group texts) is warranted. I really detest how much parenting seems to involve trying to one-up other parents.

And yet other aspects of parenting I had never even thought about have surfaced as my favorite part of the gig. Namely, hand-holding and conversing. To me, holding hands with my children as we walk somewhere—anywhere—is the most powerful experience as a mother because we are interdependent. I'm not sweating from carrying their weight, which makes us able to talk to each other. And on the occasions my kids are fed, calm, and not in need of a new diaper, I find sitting and talking with them to be surprisingly engrossing. But never once while shopping for nursery décor or reading baby name books did I ever think that holding my children's hands, or talking with them, would bring me such joy. Again, I was assuming they'd sit there motionless, staring blankly at me from under yarn bangs.

And therein lies a weakness in motherhood: We are asked to prepare for emotions for which we can't possibly prepare. Before the birth of my first daughter, so many people told me how quickly I would fall in love with my child. I heard this so much that I began to panic about my own reaction to the birth of my child. Everyone told me how it *should* go and how it went for them. But something in the back of my mind kept nagging me. I worried I wouldn't have the same feelings, at least not instantly. I made my mind up that if those emotions didn't surface immediately, I would pretend they did. But when I expressed this concern to close friends they assured me that the most profound love I would ever feel in my life would happen the instant I laid eyes on my child.

Sure, sure. But giving birth hurts, and it makes you tired, and for a few days you aren't quite sure if that's the actual size of your child's nose. That's how motherhood becomes the enemy of love. It comes prepackaged with expectations on the emotions you *should* feel, *when* you should feel them, *how* you should express them, and what it might mean if you don't. And in truth, I didn't feel that overwhelming feeling I was promised until weeks later. Which meant I spent weeks convinced I was a heartless beast.

So why is it that motherhood is so glorified? What is it that is so different, unique, or substantial from being a daughter or a wife or a friend? Maybe it's that we refuse to see motherhood as what it really is: a relationship. Because if you ask me how my relationship is with my children, that's a question I'm happy to answer. Somehow, magically, I've helped create two little people—one with my face, one with my personality—whom I cannot get enough of. And my relationships with the two of them are among the most honest and rewarding relationships of my life.

While you can debate motherhood, challenge motherhood, write about motherhood (irony fully appreciated), and put pressure on motherhood, you can't debate my relationship with my children. You can't judge our conversations. Nothing about our love is controversial. We are just a few people sharing a life together.

So I have to stop from time to time and reframe the picture of motherhood. I can't allow the trappings of the role to become the image on which I focus. The image of me on a level without my kids. That image of me soaked to the bone searching for dresses, without the input of my kids, who truly don't care (or even know) about picture day. The image of me that is clamoring to show the other mothers I also know my child's teacher's favorite color. Those aren't the images of motherhood I want to look at. They are not what determines my view of the role. But when I reframe the picture, when I look specifically at the parts of motherhood that are unique to me and my children—like when they come home from picture day to tell me all about why their nice new dresses are covered in mud and paint—I find myself in awe with the framed image of my relationship with my children. It's quite a masterpiece.

GETTING TO "YES" TAKES TIME

"Yes" is not what we think it is. We think of it as a clear and instant agreement to some offer, such as when my husband proposed—I barely let him get out the words before exclaiming, "YES!" In that moment, it seemed like a yes is quick, easy, and automatic. But that yes actually took two years of dating. The truth is, a yes is hard to discern and takes much longer to get. A no, on the other hand, is quick and clear.

During the summer I helped hire the CEO of that nonprofit, the yes took a lot of time. Months and months. There were several rounds of interviews and hours of debriefing. When we finally got to yes, it was still an enthusiastic yes. If anything, the long period of mulling made the yes all the heartier—just like the lead up to my husband's proposal. It just took the search committee a lot of time to get to yes. When we finally decided, we spent another few weeks getting the feedback (and vote) of the full board of directors. By the time we called the candidate with an offer she said, "Oh, I'm so surprised! When I hadn't heard anything I assumed it was a no." It absolutely wasn't. It was a hard-won yes that took a lot of time. But as for those early-in-the-process candidates who were a flat out "No"? They were told quickly and with clarity.

A yes takes research gathering and time. Part of your quest for your dream, whatever it may be, will require patience. This doesn't mean letting life pass you by, and it certainly doesn't mean not going forward with other projects. In fact, understanding that a yes takes a lot of time should encourage you to keep doing other stuff while you wait.

You can still wait a long time and end up with a no. But in my experience, that's far more rare. Typically, a long wait leans more in your favor. When our fertility doctor told us, "The longer you try, the more chance you have at success," I laughed because it seemed both too simplistic and incorrect. After all, the longer we tried, the more we felt it was not going to happen. But the doctor's advice turned out to be right, and also a good mantra for life. Good things really do come to those who wait because good things almost always take time. There are no overnight successes, just people who worked long and hard on their craft—be they comedians, musicians, writers, actors, athletes, and so on—and one day finally got their big break. I've submitted enough writing projects to see that a no comes back quickly, sometimes within mere minutes. There have been times I wished a "no" could have taken a bit longer, just to soften the blow. But the projects that get published take months, sometimes years, of revision and resubmissions.

The point is this: Don't mistake inaction, silence, or delays in what you want as a "no." You will clearly hear a "no." It will be loud, possibly painful, and usually quicker than you anticipated. And while nothing makes that sting less, at least you can be grateful the unknown is over. However, if you are still waiting in the wings for your "Yes!" but are met with silence, don't rule the possibility out. And above all, don't ever rule yourself out.

• • •

During my semester abroad in college, three of my friends and I signed up for a weeklong adventure tour around Scotland. This trip mostly involved hiking across the Scottish countryside and visiting castles and distilleries with twenty strangers from all over the world. The last stop on our tour was Loch Ness, where we hoped to catch a glimpse of the massive, magical monster I secretly believed was real.

As our rickety tour bus lumbered over the hills and valleys, toward the water, our tour guide, Ruthie—a short brunette with a Scottish brogue—began telling about the first time she visited Loch Ness.

She and her two best friends grew up hearing about the loch's mystical powers, powers provided by the beautiful and elusive monster, in whom the natives aggressively believe. The lore suggests that pursuing the Loch Ness monster is, in and of itself, a measure of true bravery. It is believed that to show your certainty in the monster, and your valiant efforts to find her, you should run naked into the loch. Don't think about how deep the water is (one of the deepest lakes in the world) or how cold (such deep waters can't get warm in the misty Scotland climate). Just run. Dive deep down into the endless, frigid waters, and when you come out, you come out cloaked with good fortune as a reward for your courage and faith.

Then you toast your new luck with a swig of Scotland's finest drink.

Ruthie laughed fondly as she told of how she and her friends emerged from the loch, naked and shivering, and spent the evening warming by a fire while they sipped whiskey and watched the waves carry all their bad luck out to sea. She couldn't explain how, exactly, but that night changed her life. When the dawn came and the whiskey hangover subsided, she knew she would never be the same.

She seemed lost in her memories as we pulled up to the water's edge. She turned off the engine, reached under her seat, pulled out an unopened bottle of Scotch, and glanced back at everyone on the bus.

Without looking at one another, without even uttering a word, my friends and I, in beautiful synchronization, kicked off our shoes and began unbuttoning our shirts. We were stumbling off the bus as we unzipped our pants. We hopped around on the rocks, trying to pull the socks from our feet. And on that cold, foggy Scotland day—like some beautiful, slow-motion scene in a gripping movie—we all ran toward the loch.

When my feet first hit the water, an icy chill went through my entire body in a painful jolt. Though I felt frozen, my body kept moving over the slippery, smooth pebbles that cover the loch's floor. I kept running. I ran until I was up to my neck in frigid water.

And then I dove.

Once I completely submerged my entire body in the wintery water, I popped up immediately, a little surprised to be alive. I quickly and effortlessly swam back to shore. And there was Ruthie, jumping and screaming with delight as she waved her siren bottle of Scotch in the air. She ran to us, enveloping us all in a joyful embrace. We were all leaping in the air and triumphantly high-fiving while Ruthie cracked open the bottle. As we gathered up our clothes, which had made a trail from the bus to the shore, we looked up to notice, for the first time, that the rest of the tour group was still on the bus, faces pressed against the windows, mouths agape.

In that moment, all I wanted was to make my college years last forever.

When I received a job offer to become a faculty member at the university, I couldn't have been more excited by the opportunity. That job offer, after all, was the result of an extremely long hunt.

In the midst of my dissertation research, there had been speculation around campus that a faculty position might be opening up in my field of study. At the time, it was just a rumor. For months I tried to find out more information. I'd casually ask people in the break room. I'd eavesdrop on conversations in the bathroom. I'd stand with my ear suctioned to a cup pressed up to the dean's door.

To me, the rumored position—and all the details about it that I liberally filled in myself—seemed wonderful. While I've never subscribed to the notion of a "dream job," it certainly fit many criteria for the kind of job I'd want. This mythical opportunity could allow me the challenging career I'd long desired, coupled with the flexibility I would need with a family. And it's no secret that opportunities for newly-minted PhDs are a grim fairy tale.

Over the course of two years, my life accidentally became a prolonged quest for this folkloric possibility. Despite having no factual evidence that this job would ever exist or that I'd even be considered for it, I carried on ambitiously as though it did and I would.

It wasn't as if I wasted time while I waited. I birthed and cared for a child while I finished my doctorate degree. Then I became pregnant with another child. I worked as an adjunct teacher and as a researcher on various grant-funded projects for the university. I did a fair amount of consultation work. I had the dog groomed. But I found myself refusing to settle into a permanent position. At first, I felt courageous believing in the existence of something without reason or evidence. But in the meantime, I let many other opportunities pass me by. I even turned down a gracious job offer that would have benefited my family financially, for the absurd pursuit of what was likely a mirage.

Waiting was not only making me crazy, it was making me selfish.

After more than a year of fantasizing, the rumored opening became fact. A national search was to be held to fill the role. A search can take up to a year as candidates from across the country are vetted and considered. Though I knew internal candidates are rarely chosen in academia, I applied and prepared myself for another extended wait.

Another year went by.

All the waiting created a certain level of self-doubt and depression. Well-intentioned friends kept asking whether I had heard anything, and my explanation for still waiting made me feel irrational, manic even. But eventually, just as I was about to give up, the waiting turned into progress. And the progress turned into an interview. And the interview turned into an offer. And the offer turned into a job. As I prepared to start my new role as an assistant professor, I wondered what I'm sure the Scottish have always secretly wondered: Could the monster ever be as magical as imagined?

That afternoon in Scotland—after we emerged from the water, caught our breath, and got dressed—we stumbled, fuzzy from whiskey, over to a silver Airstream parked close to shore. A sign outside read, "Loch Ness Monsters for Sale £1.00." I pounded hard on the metal door. A man, young and attractive but disheveled and crazed, swung open the door as if he himself had also been drinking.

"I want to buy a Loch Ness monster," I declared.

"Okay," he said, unimpressed with the four of us. "Come on in."

Inside we found an unmade bed with plaid flannel sheets, a hot plate, and a table cluttered with mounds of clay, googly eyes, and hundreds of Loch Ness monster figurines. I picked out one that was holding a little book and wearing a tiny pair of wire spectacles. It did, and still does, make me laugh to think of Nessie as bookish.

"So you live here?" I asked.

"Yep," he replied, running a hand through his dirty hair. "I make and sell these to raise money for my research."

"Oh?" I said, intrigued there was a purpose to the kitsch. "What do you research?"

"The Loch Ness monster," he said earnestly. "I'm trying to find her."

My friend snorted. "At a buck a piece, it's gonna take you forever."

"That may be true," he said, yawning as he scratched his beard. "But I'm crazy enough to wait."

GO GET WHAT YOU WANT

I've noticed that when people really want something, they refuse to act like they do. My good friend was contemplating whether she and her husband were ready for a baby. She bought dozens of books and borrowed some of mine, and most of our lunches together were consumed with talking about what it's like to be a mother. Then one evening, after work and over drinks, she said, "Okay, well I'm officially stopping my birth control tomorrow."

"You're finally trying!" I exclaimed, my arms outstretched to hug her.

"No, no, no!" She shook her head and put her hands up to block my embrace. "We aren't *trying*, we just aren't *preventing*."

This was my friend's attempt to act like she didn't care. But knowing her as I did, I knew she cared very much. I also knew she would spend her lunch hours Googling tips to conceive and would make sure she and her husband were having sex, facing east, at the exact moment her ovulation kit told her to. I get why my friend wanted to act like she wasn't trying for a baby. Having tried for two of my own—the first one with help from a fertility doctor—I know how crushing it can be to want something you are worried you won't get. But I urged her, and I urge you, to be open with your goals. Don't try to hide them under your defenses: "I'd be happy with a promotion, but I love the job I'm doing now." Don't bury them under your fear of rejection: "If he asks me out, great, but I love being single and am in no hurry to be in a relationship."

Look, if you really don't want the baby, or the promotion, or the significant other, that's completely fine, too. But don't feel you have to hide the fact that you want things or that you are actively *trying* for those things. Put your desires out there to the universe, your best friend, or the barista at your favorite coffeehouse if you must, because the more you own your wants, the more likely you are to get them. If you don't get them, then at least you've surrounded yourself with people who know your wishes and will be there to comfort you.

One year, while watching the Oscars, I commented to Jim how incredible it must be to learn you got nominated for an award like that. "Sure," Jim smiled, "but they knew they had been put up for nomination." Until that moment, it had never occurred to me that you have to essentially *be* nominated to *get* nominated. You have to submit materials for consideration. I'm not sure how I thought it worked; I guess I imagined that the committee just watched *every single movie* in the world and made a short list of the best performances. Much like most awards—40 Under 40, Emmys, Grammys, Tonys, the freaking Pulitzer Prize— *you* have to put yourself out there and let people know you want it. Oscar winners aren't just winners because they were passive in their own careers; they put themselves up (or allowed others to put them up) for a big award. All that fuss on stage acting like they are happy just to be nominated is only partially true; they went after it. And I guess what I want to say to you more than anything else is: Put yourself out there. Let the world know your wants. Own your excitement, talk about your fears, and be okay with saying "I'm going to try something!" You will lose 100 percent of the jobs, promotions, awards, and opportunities you don't apply for. Whatever it is you want, you got this. So go get it.

• • •

When my husband was in high school, he asked his parents if he could go to New York City during winter break. They agreed, back in the days before cell phones and Giuliani's cleanup of Times Square, to let Jim experience NYC all by himself. The jury is still out on whether this decision makes my in-laws amazing parents or outright negligent, but off their teenage boy went to the Big Apple solo.

He stayed in a cheap motel in Yonkers and awoke early every morning to ride the bus and train into the city. He spent twelve hours each day walking the streets, eating at restaurants, attending plays, and riding in taxis, before catching a late bus back to the suburb.

When Jim was a junior in college, he decided he wanted to attend film school. The best film programs were in New York City and Los Angeles. Despite having grown up in small-town Oklahoma, having lived at home all through college, and having never been to the West Coast, Jim applied to the University of Southern California and was accepted. He set out to live and attend graduate school in the south-central area of Los Angeles.

There, Jim graduated at the top of his class with a master of fine arts degree in film and television production. During his final semester, he went with some classmates to the ABC Studios lot for a guided tour of the stages. During the tour, he befriended a writers' assistant for *General Hospital*, and a few days later was offered an internship on the show. A few months following, the internship turned into a staff position, and he spent years helping write the show and even shared in a couple of Emmys.

Later, having decided to leave behind the fast-paced and outrageously expensive life in LA, Jim moved back to Oklahoma to buy a house, find a wife, and have some babies. But before he settled down, he saw an online ad seeking a television scriptwriter for the World Wrestling Federation (now the WWE). Or as Jim calls it, soap operas for sweaty men. Having long been a fan of professional wrestling, and with experience in long-form storytelling, Jim applied for, and was offered, the job.

So, despite having just bought a house in Oklahoma, he took off for Connecticut, at six feet tall and 130 pounds, to sit in a room full of seven-foot-tall, 350-pound professional wrestlers and draft their stories from week to week. At the time Jim was writing for two of the most famous wrestlers—Stone Cold Steve Austin and The Rock—and the highest rated cable show on television: *Monday Night Raw.* There sat my slender, smart, sophisticated, and soft-spoken future husband among hulking, ambitious, and powerful men, pitching ideas of how they could poetically bash each other over the head with metal folding chairs. I tell you all this to illustrate how, at every turn in his life, Jim has powered through obstacles with an abundance of confidence.

In general, I believe I have a level of confidence that gets me through most of the bigger challenges in life, too. But there are also moments of intimidation and insecurity in which I feel perhaps I've overreached my potential and outstretched my abilities.

When I was in high school, my parents insisted I enroll in advanced calculus. They had forced this on my sister and brother several years earlier, so I knew I probably wouldn't escape this absurdity. Thus, as a senior in high school, I was in class with fifteen other students who I came to understand were not there because their parents demanded it, but because they had tested extremely well and earned their seat in the classroom.

Our calculus teacher, despite being among the greatest instructors I've ever had, did one traumatizing thing: She posted our grades on the wall. And while only our social security numbers identified us, there was only ever one grade lower than an A in the entire class. So not only did I feel like the idiot in the classroom, but now a large group of really smart people had my SSN.

It took years of self-love and therapy to see that, while I didn't make an A in advanced calculus, I also didn't do horribly. In fact, I finished that course with a B, and I have gone on to have a fairly normal and productive life.

When I studied abroad during college, I felt instantly that I had overreached. Every part of leaving my home country to live for half a year in a foreign land—even an English-speaking one—was difficult. When our plane touched down in London that first day, I was full of enthusiasm and energy. But when we arrived on campus, my roommate and I were told our dorm room was not yet ready and to come back in a few hours.

She wandered off to buy stamps and toiletries, leaving me to roam the city all alone on my first day in another country. While I'd like to say that I went skipping through London drinking tea and looking for the Queen, I actually sat down on a park bench and cried. I was homesick and afraid. I was certain that I could not survive six solid months in this strange land where cars drove on the other side of the road and it rained constantly.

While I now look back on my time studying abroad with nothing but warm feelings and pleasant memories, the first few days were tough. I had stretched out my arms for this amazing adventure and felt I couldn't quite grab hold of it. But after the first couple of weeks, I began to find my rhythm. Before the month was up, I dreaded returning to the States.

And don't get me started on how much I overreached when I became a mother. Or an academic. Even several years into both I sometimes feel underqualified.

Recently, while out to dinner, I asked Jim about his time in New York, LA, and Connecticut. Mostly, I wanted to know how he was able to repeatedly put himself into situations in which he was clearly reaching beyond his potential. How did he manage to always extend his arms and grab the things that were just beyond his reach? And, more important, why did he never see himself as overreaching?

He shrugged. "In high school, before I left for New York, I read something in a travel book about how to survive as a tourist in the city," he recalled. "Guess it just stuck with me."

"Oh?" I asked. "What did it say?"

"When you reach your destination, you've earned the right to be there."

• • •

You may be the hands on your back, pushing you forward. But you may also be the hands on your chest, holding you back. Release yourself. Quiet your doubts, hush your fears, and silence your insecurities. Listen instead to your dreams. They sound like crazy delusions that are constantly whispering in your ear—noise you keep ignoring. Don't tune them out; turn them up. They are in your head and heart for a reason. Listen to them and go forth. Forget about the ideal image, forget about perfection. Just go. Run headfirst into whatever it is you want. And remember: Just like how you get through the airport faster when you don't have to check luggage, the less baggage you allow yourself to carry, the faster you will reach your destination.

The Closer
for TACTIC FIVE

- **Allow** yourself to be motivated by your wildest dreams.

- **Realize** that being perfect is not a goal. Imagine what you could be if you strove for excellence, instead.

- **Avoid** focusing on your enemy; the second you outsmart it, it will shift its shape.

- **Understand** that getting to "YES!" takes time. If you haven't heard "NO," assume you're still in the game.

- **Recognize** when you've hit your goals. They don't often look exactly as we pictured them in our head, but the clearer the image, the more real it is.

- **Nominate** yourself for whatever it is you want: a job, a house, a spouse, a promotion, an award, an adventure. Raise your hand and say, "I want that."

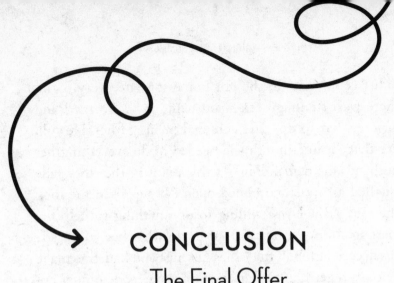

CONCLUSION
The Final Offer

As I draw to a close, I want to make one thing very clear: Negotiations only work if there is a counteroffer. That's true with real estate, salary, and life. It is especially true when you negotiate with yourself. But sometimes we get in a tricky spot where we are negotiating away our money, talent, or time and effort to an empty void. We aren't countering back.

My college friend Jade got married just after graduation and moved far away. Five years later she was divorced. She came through town one night and we met for dinner. After reliving all our grand (and occasionally drunken) times in college, she opened up about her marriage. She said that after a few years, her husband had started complaining about various aspects of their relationship. She didn't cook enough, she got home too late every night, there wasn't enough sex—you name it. Concerned and unsure what to do, Jade confided in her father. He told her that for one month she needed to do everything her husband was demanding. At this point in the story Jade laughed as my jaw dropped open. "It surprised me too," she said. "But I was willing to do anything to help my marriage." So she had set out to do what her father advised: correct for all the issues her husband had. She made a point to get home after work on time, made dinner every night, and amped up the intimacy. One month later, her husband came back with new issues. He didn't like her friends, how she wore her hair, that they hadn't had a baby—you name it. Jade's father had pushed her to comply because he had suspected what she came to see: Her husband wasn't putting anything on the table. There was no negotiation; she was giving everything, but getting nothing in return.

A few years ago, I accidently found a house I loved. How do you accidently find houses, you ask? You obsessively check the Zillow app while waiting in checkout lines. You can accidently find hundreds of homes this way. Though we had been casually looking for houses, we weren't quite ready to move. Regardless, my husband and I decided this house was at least worth a tour. It was priced at more than we wanted to spend, but what harm could come of going to the open house? While there, we quickly realized we had to have this place, and we started to sweat because we felt the house was way overpriced. I asked the agent how the sellers had arrived at their price. He laughed, waved his hand, and said, "The family is incredibly motivated, and this price is too high." Armed with that insight—and noting the many months the house had sat on the market—we put together a good offer, though it was contingent on the sale of our current home. We got word that the sellers wouldn't review our offer until our house was listed. In less than twenty-four hours, our house was on the market. Then we were told the sellers wouldn't look at our offer until we had an offer on our house. Twelve hours later we had four bids, including two above asking price, but still no word on our offer to the sellers. Several days passed before they came back, not with a counteroffer, but with this pithy prompt: "Offer more." After hearing that, we walked away. It was clear we were giving everything but getting nothing in return.

Be wary any time you find yourself without a counteroffer. Don't fool yourself into believing you are in a negotiation if it is actually a hostage situation, and don't hold yourself hostage. When a thought enters your head like, "I'm not experienced enough," or "I'm not worthy enough," or "Maybe when my hair grows out a little," go ahead and counter back to that. I am experienced enough. I am worthy enough. I will try parting it in the middle.

The point is, when it comes to negotiating with ourselves, we can get in situations where we don't allow ourselves to counter. But those counteroffers help move you toward your goal. Put them out there and let yourself build up to where you want to be. Your initial offer might be, "I want to move to Spain and be a millionaire." And if you push that aside quickly because it seems too outrageous, and you don't even allow yourself a counter, you will probably never make it to Spain. But if you counter with, "I will spend six months in Spain and work on building a business," you are more likely to get back up to your initial offer. When you realize you're lowballing yourself, drive the value back up with a solid counter. But never, ever, stop negotiating.

Make offers for all the things you want: the job, the friends, the significant other, the house, the kids, the travel, the adventures, and even the way you love and treat yourself. Go after it all and entertain other offers along the way. They may not be all you want at first, but a little negotiating can get you there. Don't undervalue yourself and all your wants. Don't walk away from a big dream because it seems unachievable; give yourself some negotiating room to get there. And if ever you feel stuck—in life, love, or work—remember that every aspect can be renegotiated. Revisit your terms when needed.

We are all negotiating for the lives we want, what we are willing to give, and what we need to get. I'm grateful for the students who have shared their negotiations with me. I am proud of them for putting themselves out there—both in service to others and in demand for themselves. The more they ask for, the more they get. And I'm grateful for my daughters, two little spitfires who swarm around me daily, negotiating for the lives—and snacks—they want. The more they ask for, the more they get. I rely on the wisdom of those demanding, opinionated, negotiating daughters—asking for a cookie to put on the kitchen table until later—because they have taught me the most valuable lessons I've ever learned as a woman: Ask for everything you want. Find a way to have it all. And leave nothing on the table.

ACKNOWLEDGMENTS

This book, like everything in life, was a team effort. I'm forever grateful for the team of people who helped make this happen. First, to my ridiculously cool and wonderful agent, Carly Watters, you have, quite literally, changed my life. To my kind and encouraging editor, Stephanie Knapp, thank you for choosing this book, for choosing me, and for the care you took with my words and emotions. To Jeff Martin, you have made Tulsa a literary destination, which truly makes it a Magic City. Thank you for the support you've given me as a small part of that.

I must also thank the most influential person in my professional life, Dr. Alisa Hicklin Fryar. I'm not sure what to call you: coworker, supervisor, mentor, ally? I know what you prefer, of course, which is *friend*. You helped me pursue—and thrive in—a career I could never have dreamed of. And if that weren't enough, you fight hard every day to make sure I focus on the right things, ignore the petty things, and enjoy the ride. They say empowered women empower other women. Thanks for empowering me to a point where I'm able to empower others.

Also, a special thanks to the University of Oklahoma–Tulsa president John Schumann. You are an empowering leader for the faculty on your campus, but you are also an inspiration to those of us trying to have careers that don't fit the typical mold. You set the bar and the tone.

And, of course, thank you, thank you, thank you to my students. Your quest for a better world, and better selves, is inspiring. The discussions we've shared in the classroom and the conversations we've had in my office are the greatest honor of my career. Thank you for sharing your time with me. Special thanks to Taylor Potter, Lauren McKinney, Trenton Kissee, Maggie Den Harder, and Piper Wolfe for being sounding boards and champions to my ideas. Your excitement kept me excited. And endless thanks to former student and current friend, Cassandra Rigsby. You were the first person to let me think I might have some advice to give.

Thank you to my mom and dad, for being dreamers in their own right, setting an expectation for your kids to dream big, too. Thank you to my sister for being my best friend and for answering the phone every time I call. Even really late at night.

Above all else, I must emphatically thank the members of Team Morgan. Lowery, you are my heart. London, you are my soul. I appreciate the strength, affection, curiosity, and determination you both possess. Thank you both for teaching me the beautiful art of negotiating.

And finally, to Jim. You are, and forever will be, the highlight of my life. Also, we are out of milk.

REFERENCES

Ahmad, S. (2017). Family or future in the academy? *Review of Educational Research,* 87 (1), 204–239.

Aitken, S., Lyons, M., & Jonason, P. (2013). Dads or cads? Women's strategic decisions in the mating game. *Personality and Individual Differences,* 55 (2013), 118–122.

Avey, J. B., Reichard, R., Luthans, F., & Mhatre, K. H. (2011). Meta-analysis of the impact of positive psychological capital on employee attitudes, behaviors, and performance. *Human Resource Development Quarterly,* 22 (2), 127–152.

Beck, C., Prosser, P., & Wallace, R. (2005). Trying again to fail-first. Conference Paper: International Workshop on Constraint Solving and Constraint Logic Programming. Lecture Notes in Computer Science, 3419. Springer, Berlin, Heidelberg.

Borzelleca, D. (2012, February 16). The male-female ratio in college. *Forbes.*

Brachinger, H. W., Gysler, M., Brown, M., & Schubert, R. (1999). Financial decision-making: Are women really more risk averse? *The American Economic Review*, 92 (2).

Brems, C., Baldwin, M., Davis, L., & Namyniuk, L. (1994). The imposter syndrome as related to teaching evaluations and advising relationships of university faculty members. *Journal of Higher Education*, 65 (2), 183–193.

Brown, Brene (2015). Daring greatly. Avery.

Buser, T., & Yuan, H. (2016). Do women give up competing more easily? Evidence from the lab and the Dutch Math Olympiad. Tibergen Institute. University of Amsterdam.

Carver, C. S., Scheier, M., & Segerstrom, S. (2010). Optimism. *Clinical Psychology Review*, 30, 879–889.

Christopher, K. (2012). Extensive mothering: Employed mothers' construction of the good mother. *Gender and Society*, 26 (1), 73–96.

Cialdini, R. & Goldstein, N. (2004). Social influence: Compliance and conformity.

Deustch, M., & Gerard, H. B. (1955). A study of normative and informative social influences upon individual judgement. *Abnormal Social Psychology*, 51, 629–636.

Dunkley, D. M., Zuroff, D. C., & Blankstein, K. R. (2003). Self-critical perfectionism and daily affect: Dispositional and situational influences on stress and coping. *Journal of Personality and Social Psychology*, 84 (1), 234–252.

Ely, R., Stone, P., & Ammerman, C. (2014). Rethink what you "know" about high-achieving women. *Harvard Business Review*. December.

Fink, B., Klappauf, Brewer, G., & Shackelford, T. (2013). Female physical characteristics and intra-sexual competition in women. *Personality and Individual Differences. Elsevier* 58 (2014), 138–141.

Flynn, F. (2008, July 1). If you want something, just ask for it. *Stanford Business*. Retrieved from https://www.gsb.stanford.edu/insights/francis-flynn-if-you-want-something-ask-it.

Frost, R. O., Marten, P., Lahart, C. M., & Rosenblate, R. (1990). The Dimensions of Perfectionism. *Cognitive Therapy and Research*, 14 (5), 449–468.

Furst, H. (2016). Handling rejection as failure: Aspiring writers getting the rejection slip. *Valuation Studies*, 4 (2), 153–176.

Gerson, K. (2010). *Hard choices: How women decide about work, careers, and motherhood*. Berkley: University of California Press.

Gottman, J., Schwartz Gottman, J., & DeClaire, J. (2006). 10 lessons to transform your marriage. New York: Crown Publishers.

Haralick, R. M., & Elliott, G. L. (1980). Increasing tree search efficiency for constraint satisfaction problems. *Artificial Intelligence*, 14, 263–314.

Henderson, R. (2016, September 29). How powerful is the status quo? *Psychology Today*. Retrieved from https://www.psychologytoday.com/blog/after-service/201609/how-powerful-is-status-quo-bias.

Hock, H. (2008). The pill and the college attainment of American women and men. Working Paper, Washington, D.C.: Mathematica Policy Research.

Ievleva, L., & Ovlick, T. (1991). Mental links to enhanced healing: An exploratory study. *The Sports Psychologist*, 5, 25–40.

Kahneman, D., & Tversky, A. (1979). Prospect theory: An analysis of decision under risk. *Econometrica*, 47, 263–291.

Losada, M., & Heaphy, E. (2004). The role of positivity and connectivity in the performance of business teams. *American Behavioral Scientist*, 47 (6), 740–765.

Magnet, S. (2017). Are you my mother? Understanding feminist therapy with Alison Bechdel. *Women and Therapy*, 40 (1–2), 207–227.

Morrison, E. W., & Milliken, F. J. (2003). Speaking up, remaining silent: The dynamics of voice and silence in organizations. *Journal of Management Studies*, 40 (6), 1354–1358.

Moss-Racusin, C. (2011). Understanding women's self-promotion detriments. (Doctoral dissertation). Retrieved from https://doi.org/doi:10.7282/T3V1243Z. Rutgers University.

Neck, C. P., & Manz, C. C. (1992). Thought self-leadership: The influence of self-talk and mental imagery on performance. *Journal of Organizational Behavior*, 13 (7), 681–699.

Pagnan, C., & Wadsworth, S. (2015). Graduate students' perceptions of the prospects for combining career and family: The role of academic program and gender. *The Journal of the Professoriate*, 8 (1), 22–52.

Paquette, D. (2016, July 7). Young women are still less likely to negotiate a job offer. But why? *The Washington Post*.

Ratliff, K. (2013). Gender differences in implicit self-esteem following a romantic partner's success or failure. *Journal of Personality and Social Psychology*, 105 (4), 688–702.

Robinson, K. J., Mayer, S., Allen, A. B., Terry, M., Chilton, A., & Leary, M. (2016). Resisting self-compassion: Why are some people opposed to being kind to themselves? *Self and Identity*, 5 (5), 505–524.

Samuelson, W., & Zechaueser, R. (1988). Status quo bias in decision-making. *Journal of Risk and Uncertainty*, 1 (1), 7–59.

Sandberg, S. (2013). *Lean in*. Knopf.

Schmich, M. (1997, June 1). Advice, like youth, probably just wasted on the young. *Chicago Tribune*.

Schmitt, D. P., & Buss, B. M. (2001). Human mate poaching: Tactics and temptations for short-term mates: What, whether, and why. *Journal of Personality and Social Psychology*, 90, 468–489.

Shapiro, M., Ingols, C., & Blake-Beard, S. (2011). Using power to influence outcomes: Does gender matter? *Journal of Management Education*, 35 (5), 713–748.

Sonfield, A., Hasstedt, K., Kavanaugh, M., & Anderson, R. (2013). The social and economic benefits of women's ability to determine whether and when to have children. *Guttmacher Institute*. University of Michigan.

Stoeber, J., Hutchfield, J., & Wood, K. V. (2008). Perfectionism, self-efficacy, and aspiration level: Differential effects of perfectionistic striving and self-criticism after success and failure. *Personality and Individual Differences*, 45 (4), 323–327.

References

Tversky, A., & Kahneman, D. (1974). Judgment under uncertainty: Heuristics and biases. *Science,* 185 (4158), 1124–1131.

Wade, T. J., & McCrae, S. (1999). Intrasexual competition and contrast effects on men's self-ratings of attractiveness and social ascendancy: Status, physical fitness, or looks. *Psychology, Evolution, and Gender,* 1, 229–243.

ABOUT THE AUTHOR

Dr. Meg Myers Morgan is an assistant professor at the University of Oklahoma and the director of graduate programs in public administration and nonprofit management on the OU-Tulsa campus. Meg's collection of essays, *Harebrained: It Seemed Like a Good Idea at the Time,* won the gold medal for humor from the Independent Publisher Book Awards (IPPY). She gave a TED Talk, "Negotiating for Your Life," for TEDxOU in 2016. She speaks publicly about recruiting and retaining talent, negotiating in work and life, and developing women as leaders. Meg holds a PhD and an MPA from the University of Oklahoma, a degree in English and creative writing with honors from Drury University, and is certified in executive and leadership coaching from Columbia University. She lives in Tulsa with her husband and their two young daughters.